Read

The Living Room Bed

Birthing, Healing, and Dying in Traditional Appalachia

BY

PEGGY ANN SHIFFLETT

AWARD WINNING AUTHOR

2-21-18

To Margaret,
I hope you enjoy my stories!

Peggy Ann Shifflett

ISBN: 978-1-4507-0720-6

Other books by this author:

The Red Flannel Rag: Memories of An Appalachian Childhood

Mom's Family Pie: Memories of Food Traditions and Family in Appalachia

Printed and bound in the United States of America by:
McClung Companies, 500 Commerce Ave., Waynesboro, VA 22980

Orders should be sent to:
Peggy A. Shifflett
700 Cherrywood Rd.
Salem, VA 24153
Phone: 540-387-9154
Email: pshiffle@radford.edu

Acknowledgements

This book is a result of the encouragement of several people. My cousins, Charles Morris, Arvona McMullen, and Betty Morris Fleming supported me and gave me ideas. Carol Stuart encouraged me and read a very early draft to note numerous improper uses of "sit," "set," and "sat." Eve Deegan read and edited an early draft, offered helpful comments, and told me to keep on working on it. Scottie Pritchard offered her home and encouragement in the planning stages.

Manila Cannaday, Arlene Scott, Peggy Harris, Pat Bussey, and Shirley Ingram sat with me for many hours as I asked questions. Peggy and Pat provided pictures to illustrate certain points. My brothers, John and Warnie, and my sister, Brenda, helped with pictures, dates, and information. Aunt Ethel and Uncle Shirley (1916-2007) were incredible resources for pictures and great stories. Mary Morris Turner and her sons Gary and Dennis provided pictures. I am grateful for their help. Debbie Pryor provided pictures. I will always be thankful to Lori Bennett, a distant cousin, who spent many hours researching the families of Hopkins Gap. Her work has been very valuable to me.

I am deeply grateful to the readers of my first two books, The Red Flannel Rag: Memories of an Appalachian Childhood and Mom's Family Pie: Memories of Food Traditions and Family in Appalachia. Many of them asked me to write another book, and this work is a response to those requests. I greatly appreciate Dr. Stevan Jackson for using The Red Flannel Rag in his Appalachian culture classes and for his review of my books. I thank the booksellers, the librarians, and the historical societies for their encouragement. To the men and women on both sides of my family, who allowed me to ask a million questions, I owe a great debt. Finally, I want to thank Anita Firebaugh. She did the final editing of this book. She asked the right questions and offered great suggestions where needed. I thank you, Anita.

Dedicated

to

Dad and Mom

Norman Shifflett, 1919-1994

Myrtle Morris Shifflett, 1920-2001

My brother

Larry Norman Shifflett, 1942-2006

My nephew

Kent Anthony Rhodes, 1964-2009
(short lived, always and forever loved)

Table of Contents

Page

Acknowledgements i

Dedication. iii

Preface. 1

Introduction 5

PART I: **ARRIVING ON EARTH IN THE "LIVING ROOM" BED** 21

Chapter 1—Being Born 25

Chapter 2—Mom's Babies 31

Chapter 3—Midwives of Hopkins Gap 41

Chapter 4—Gender Mattered 53

Chapter 5—Being One of Many 63

Chapter 6—Birth Order. 71

Chapter 7—Many Aunts and Uncles 89

PART II: **GROWING INDEPENDENT OF THE "LIVING ROOM" BED** 101

Chapter 8—Graduating to the Sleeping Loft 103

Chapter 9—Recovering from Childhood Illnesses. 117

Chapter 10—Practical Lessons About Work 135

PART III: **ESTABLISHING A "LIVING ROOM" BED** 155

Chapter 11—Searching for a Mate 159

Chapter 12—Courtship and Marriage 167

PART IV: **SAYING GOODBYE IN THE "LIVING ROOM" BED** 175

Chapter 13—Death along the Appalachians 177

Chapter 14—My First Real Experiences with Death 187

EPILOGUE 197

FOOTNOTES 201

Preface

My purpose in writing this book is to present and preserve the traditional events surrounding the various stages of the family life cycle in selected areas of Appalachia. I want to show that the "living room" bed was central to all of family life. The folks that I gathered information from came from a variety of small communities along the Allegheny and Blue Ridge Appalachian Ranges. I interviewed people from Washington, Grayson, Patrick, and Franklin Counties–the far southwestern part of the state–and in Rockingham and Augusta Counties–the far northeastern part of Virginia. I interviewed people from selected areas along the Interstate 81 corridor, which includes Salem, Roanoke, and Covington, Virginia. I conducted a small number of interviews with folks who grew up in West Virginia and Kentucky. I did not interview in other sections of Appalachia such as the coal mining regions or the southern foothills of Georgia, North Carolina, or Tennessee.

I structured my interviews around the phases of the life cycle that we all have had to pass through in order to be here today to read this book. We all were born in some fashion. Some of us were brought into this world at home in a "living room" bed with the help of a midwife. If not, we remember someone who was born in this manner–our parents or grandparents.

We older folks were usually one of many children born to our parents. We had to accept the fact that the new baby would replace us as the "special" child when it arrived. Many of the folks I interviewed indicated that it was nice to have many brothers and sisters because that meant a lot of first cousins to form teams and play games. Yet, there was a pervasive resentment built into the fact that their time as a "special" child was short-lived. Most interviewees admitted a subtle dislike of the youngest child in the family. They said that this child was "spoiled rotten" and they often resented him or her. Because many of the youngest children were born at the end of the mother's reproductive cycle, folks called them "menopause" babies. That label carried an expected set of behaviors along with it.

Both male and female experiences prepared them for their future roles–nurturer and caregiver for the females and conqueror, explorer, leader, warrior, or protector for the males. Female experiences tended to happen closer to home. Females played with dolls and jump ropes. Many female games included concerns about maturing into a woman. The games involved future marriages, the number of children they might have, and which boy in the community would be their lifelong companion. The settings for female experiences were on the back porch, the bedroom, or under a tree in the yard, preferably a tree that was easy to climb.

While marriage and childbirth were a constant theme in the thoughts of females, the men that I interviewed never talked about their childhood thoughts on marriage or children. When asked, they indicated that they "knew it would happen someday," but they didn't think much about it.

Male experiences tended to be such things as playing cowboys and Indians, soldiers, building forts, pretend hunting, fishing, and chopping down trees. These experiences required boys to stray far from the confines of home and family, and parents allowed them to wander off for an entire day.

All of us who grew up before "baby shots" experienced childhood epidemics of the measles, mumps, and chicken pox. We all caught an occasional flu bug, or had falls that resulted in broken bones, cuts or bruises. When those occasions needing attention came up, we returned to the "living room" bed for special care from moms, grandmas, and aunts.

When asked about death, both men and women indicated that death was all around them as they were growing up. Many had lost a sibling while they were still children. Some had lost a parent; and most had lost their grandparents at a very young age–often before their own birth.

Women interviewees talked about pet ducks and cats that died and described the funerals they and their friends planned for each one. One woman interviewee described how her parents were friends with a funeral director. When they went to visit at night, she and the daughter of the funeral director went downstairs to the funeral parlor to play. They climbed in and out of caskets, touched the dead bodies they found there, and went into the embalming room. Men talked about hunting and killing animals for food; they indicated that death was a natural end to life.

The experiences that I describe in this book occurred before modern medicine, television, and the internet. Some folks in my generation experienced what I describe in this book; others learned about the "olden days" from parents and grandparents. I hope that my older readers will enjoy returning to an earlier part of their life; and my younger readers will compare their own life cycle events in the days of modern medicine, television, and the internet with their parents' and grandparents' life cycle events.

Introduction

All Around the House

. . . home just seems a provisional claim, a designation you make upon a place, not one it makes on you. A certain set of buildings, a glimpsed, smudged window-view . . . a musty aroma sniffed when you were a child, all of which come crowding in upon your latter-day senses–those are pungent things and vivid, even consoling . . .

Richard Ford

The "Living Room" Bed

The "living room" bed, an item of furniture commonly found in Appalachian Mountain homes, was necessary for Appalachian families to carry out their life cycle events. Marriage consummation, conception, birth, healing, and death all occurred in the "living room" bed. It sat in a corner and the wife kept it neatly made up during the day. She did not allow the children to sit or play on the bed. The husband and wife slept in the "living room" bed every night unless a major life cycle event was occurring. As a part her duties, the woman of the house climbed out of bed during the night to add wood or coal to the living room stove to keep the fire burning and the house warm.

Pregnancies occurred in the "living room" bed, and, nine

months later when the birthing pains started, the husband brought in the midwife or doctor. Then the "living room" bed became the "birthing" bed. After the birth occurred, the new mother stayed in the "living room" bed for nine days while she nursed the new baby and allowed her womb to "settle back into place." While the "living room" bed was the birthing and nursing bed, the husband slept elsewhere in the house.

The "living room" bed became a "sick" bed when someone in the family came down with any of the maladies that could strike a person in those days. Mountain people suffered from cuts, broken bones, pneumonia, and influenza. Children contracted measles, mumps, whooping cough, and chicken pox, diseases then not warded off by childhood immunizations. When the end of life came for a family member, the "living room" bed became a "nursing" bed and eventually a "death" bed. Elderly people died from many causes, the same as they do today. Some lingered for months and even years while being cared for by family members. The thought of placing them in a nursing home did not exist in most Appalachian communities.

A few elderly people practiced a type of euthanasia and announced that they were tired and that it was time for them to go. The elderly woman who chose to die in this manner removed the clothing that symbolized her work–her bonnet, her apron, her dress, stockings, and shoes. She put on a cotton nightcap, and a long flannel nightgown, which represented rest at the end of the day. She lay down in the "living room" bed. The elderly man took off his denim overalls, work shirt, shoes, and socks. He remained in his long underwear that he wore when he lay down to rest at night as he lay in the "living room" bed. Family members kept the dying elderly family member clean and fed until the end of his or her life arrived.

The "Big Rocker"

A large rocking chair sat near the "living room" bed. Families referred to it by different names. Some called it "Mama's" rocker, but most of the time it was called the "big rocker." Whatever it was called, children knew they should not climb into this chair. It was not for them; and, should they get near it or touch it, a mother's voice would yell out, "Don't you dare rock that chair with no one in it. That's bad luck and somebody in the family will die."

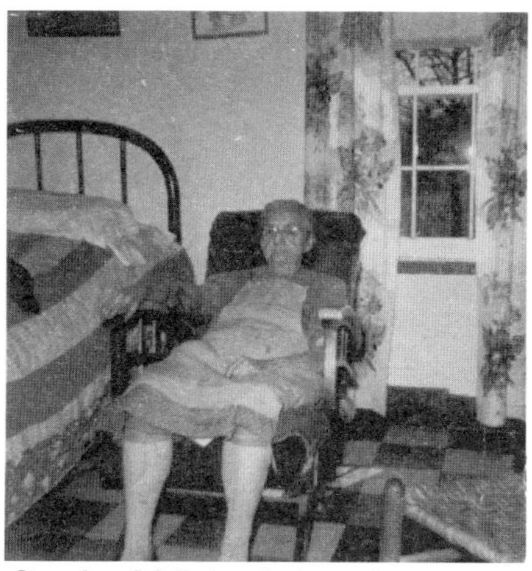

Grandma Molly is enjoying a short rest on the rocking chair beside the "living room" bed. A split-bottom chair sits nearby.

The "big rocker" was used at each stage of the life cycle. During the birth of a new baby, the midwife or female attendant used it for three days after the birth to rock the new baby. After the new mother took over the care of her baby, she sat in the "big rocker" for nursing and bonding with the tiny new family member.

When a child came down with an illness or a childhood disease, the mother put him or her in the "living room" bed. Sometimes the pain or fever was too much for the child to bear without some tender-loving nurturance. At these difficult times, the mother took the child in her arms and rocked him or her to sleep in the "big rocker." When the elderly family member was sick and dying, the preacher would come to visit and pray over the patient. The preacher always sat in the "big rocker" near the "living room" bed until he completed his visit.

Other than the "living room" bed and the "big rocker," the

only places to sit in the living room were three or four split bottom chairs. Sometimes small, less important rocking chairs provided seating for visitors and family members. They came for Sunday dinner or they came to visit a new baby or the sick or dying family members as they lay in the "living room" bed.

Beyond the "Living Room" Bed

From the steep ridges and hills of far Southwest Virginia to the mountainous borders of the Shenandoah Valley of Virginia, homesteads were similar in material culture and astonishingly similar in daily uses of the material aspects of the homestead. For example, children who grew up in the Appalachian Mountains lived in houses that varied somewhat in terms of shape or style. However, there were similar features with all houses that allowed a fairly common everyday life from one end of the mountains to another.

◆◆◆◆◆◆◆◆◆◆◆◆◆◆◆◆◆◆◆◆◆◆◆◆◆◆◆◆◆◆◆◆◆

Material Culture . . .

Material culture is a term used to describe the objects produced by human beings, including buildings, structures, monuments, tools, weapons, utensils, furniture, art, and indeed any physical item created by a society. As such, material culture is the main source of information about the past from which sociologists and anthropologists can understand how a society lived. In the context of this writing, it is possible to understand family relationships and community in traditional Appalachia by examining and explaining the purpose of commonly found physical objects such as the "living room" bed, the front and back porches, the outbuildings on the mountain homestead, and the kitchen.

◆◆◆◆◆◆◆◆◆◆◆◆◆◆◆◆◆◆◆◆◆◆◆◆◆◆◆◆◆◆◆◆◆

Some children were reared in log cabins that had sheltered several generations before them. Other children grew up in houses that were built on the sides of ridges on wooden stilts or rock foundations. Often these were two-story houses with the second story consisting of a sleeping loft with a low ceiling.

This log cabin provided shelter for several generations of the Lam family including my step-grandmother, Ivy Lam, until she died in 1984.

As the years passed by, families built larger two-story homes with partitioned bedrooms upstairs. The tools for building were simple–a hammer, a square, and a handsaw. I recall my mother pointing out a large, two-story house in Hopkins Gap that her father, John Wesley Morris, built for his family. She said, "Look at that house. My daddy built it with only a hammer, a saw, and a square. You can see that the windows are crooked." As I grew older, I looked at that house when we visited Uncle Shirley and Aunt Ethel. For sure, the windows were sitting crooked; but the house was a great improvement over the previous homes where Grandpa and Grandma Morris resided with their twelve living children. I never knew my grandfather, John Wesley Morris. However, when I looked

This home on stilts was built by my paternal grandparents, Austin and Molly Shifflett. They built it on land in Hopkins Gap that was owned by Austin's father, Banks Shifflett.

Pictured here is John William Bussey and Elizabeth Saul Bussey of Franklin County, Virginia, with the youngest of their ten children The Bussey's raised all of their children in this home in the background.

at the house that he built with simple tools, I felt close to him. At that age, I couldn't put a label on my feelings. Now I know that he worked hard and cared for his large family. I know that I am connected to him. As I ponder him as an adult, I wonder if I inherited from him my ability to see a structure in my mind and then build it.

Outside the House

While the style of the houses varied, there were some common features outside the house, such as a vegetable garden, cats and dogs, chickens, cows, and often guineas. Most houses had outbuildings such as corncribs and meat houses. Each house had a cellar–sometimes under the house and accessible by a door and steps on the outside. Other houses had cellars a short distance from the house that were dug back into a dirt bank and covered with a roof. Often the meat house building sat on top of the cellar.

Aunt Lena (front left), Grandma Molly, and a visitor from Gospel Hill Mennonite Church are standing at the front porch railing. This railing was not built for beauty as railings are today. As the rough boards testify, it was built for protection from accidentally falling off the porch.

The Porches. The porches were a very important part of mountain homes. Posts held up porch roofs. Usually each house had two porches–the "front" porch ran across the front of the house and gave access to the front door and the "back" porch ran across the back or side of the house allowing access to the back door. The back porch, just off the kitchen, provided space for many items that represented the seasonal flow of mountain life.

If the house was built up on stilts, a banister was placed around the outside of the porch floor to protect children and the elderly from falling. A set of stairs from the side yard provided access to the porch and the front door. The front porch was always equipped with several chairs for sitting while enjoying the fresh air on spring and fall evenings. Often a swing was hung on one end of the porch. The porch swing served as a resting place where one might stir up a breath of fresh air on a hot summer evening. Family and community history was passed on to youngsters as they cuddled under the arm of an older family member. The swing moved like a pendulum–back and forth, back and forth–propelled by the toes of a foot as they rhythmically touched and pushed off the porch floor. My Aunt Goldie sat on the porch swing with her arm around me as she grieved her young husband, Rob, who died from complications of gall bladder surgery. It was the fall of 1946. I was five years old. As silent tears rolled down her cheeks, she stared at Little North Mountain and the gateway to Hopkins Gap where she and Rob grew up and married. "Rob built this swing for me," she told me. "I loved him from the moment I laid eyes on him," she whispered into the cool evening air.

The back porch was very utilitarian. Here is where the first steps in food processing occurred; e.g., bean stringing, pea hulling, corn husking, cherry seeding and cutting potatoes for planting. Sometimes screen or glass closed in the back porch so that flies and other insects would not hover over the food that was processed there. In the fall and winter, it was cool enough on the back porch to store leftovers such as pinto beans until they were heated for the next meal. The back porch, in these instances, served as a place for food processing, food storage, refrigeration in appropriate weather, and the garbage dump–the slop bucket.

The Slop Bucket . . .

The preference for pork over beef was useful to the mountain family in another way. Hogs served not only as a source of food; they were also a very convenient garbage disposal. All table scraps, whey from making cottage cheese, corn husks, pea hulls, cherry seeds, strawberry caps, fruit and vegetable peelings, bad tomatoes, and everything else once edible were dumped into a "slop" bucket. At all times, a "slop" stick was kept in the slop bucket for stirring as garbage was added to the mix. As I recall, we didn't fuss too much because the slop bucket was a very necessary part of our life.

In most mountain homes, the slop bucket was very smelly depending on the season of the year. During the winter months, the slop bucket sat near the kitchen stove. Table scraps were thrown into the bucket and later fed to the hogs. Winter slop didn't have the same ingredients. It had more potato peelings, scrapings from plates, left over gravy, thus more grease.

In the summer time, the slop bucket sat on the back porch mainly because of the smell of the slop. Summer afforded a much greater variety of discarded fruits and vegetables–some acidic and others not. The combination, along with the blistering heat of July and August, rendered a boiling, fermenting, sour smell that polluted the fresh mountain air that tried to waft its way onto the back porch. Anytime the back door was opened, the stench crept into the kitchen where Mom was cooking, baking, or otherwise making some delicious food. The only thing that saved the hogs from dying from the rotten food and us from gagging ourselves to death was the fact that the slop bucket was emptied in the hog trough twice each day just before the slop became a deadly mixture.

Pat from Franklin County, Virginia told me, "The slop bucket was the easiest way to get rid of table scraps. My momma just stepped out of the kitchen door and scraped each plate into the bucket. We children knew not to bother the slop bucket and to never think about playing with the slop stick. We knew what it was for and that we shouldn't touch it."

Each morning and evening until about September, my dad stirred a portion of bran and shorts into the slop bucket and carried it up the hill to the hog pen. The weight of the bucket was obvious in his later years. He had to stop along the path to catch his breath several times and to rest before trudging on with the heavy load.

After we got our bathroom in the house in 1969, Dad moved the outside toilet up the hill and set it beside the hog pen. He stored his bran and shorts and corn meal in the two-hole outhouse and mixed the slop near the hog pen.

From September until the third weekend in November, he stirred in a portion of corn meal (or "chop" as it was called in Patrick County, Virginia) to get the hogs rolling fat for butchering. No matter what he was stirring into the slop, the smell would take your breath away.

Occasionally if the slop bucket started smelling foul, Mom would set it around the corner of the porch where the breezes carried the smell away from the house. She often did this in the winter and then forgot to bring the bucket in for the night. Of course, it froze and Dad couldn't mix it up for the hogs the next morning. Getting the slop thawed enough for the hogs to eat it was accompanied by some of the worst fights I ever heard between Mom and Dad–the kind of fights that woke me from a dead early morning sleep.

After the hog butchering in November, the table scraps and peelings would have become a problem except for my ingenious mother. Because she wanted her chickens to start producing eggs earlier than anyone else's did, she poured the contents of the slop bucket into a "cleaner" pan. She placed the pan of slop on the kitchen stove each morning to heat it. She fed the warm slop to her chickens. The process created a distinct and foul odor throughout the house.

Just like Pat said above, when my siblings and I were growing up, my mom and dad had some control over our behavior; thus, I don't remember any of us falling into the slop bucket or getting in trouble for playing with the slop stick. However, when the grandchildren and great-grandchildren started arriving on earth, it was as if they could not stand still or keep their fingers off anything they saw.

They were constantly chasing each other through the house out onto the back porch and falling into the slop bucket. One of them would yell into the kitchen, "Grandma, Curt fell in the slop bucket" or "Grandma, Kent just slapped me on the shoulder with the slop stick." Mom would just pull them out of the slop, take off their clothes, and plop them into a tub of warm water or wipe the slop off their shoulders. It really irked me that they never got their ass whipped for falling in the slop bucket and playing with the slop stick. My ass would still be blistered if I had fallen into that mess.

The slop bucket turned out to be one of my many measures of the double standard for children and grandchildren. Because we all lived on top of each other, Mom and Dad frowned on my brothers and sisters when they tried to make their grandchildren behave; thus, a whole generation of hellions replaced my well-disciplined generation that had to sneak around in the woods to do our deviant behaviors. With this change in discipline, exemplified by the consequences of falling in the slop bucket and the invention of store-bought toys, well-behaved and creative children went straight to hell.

◆ ◆

In some instances, houses did not have a "back" porch. Great Uncle Joe's house in Hopkins Gap had only one porch across the front of the house.

Joe and Millie Morris' front porch served the purposes of both the back and front porch. The family members placed chairs on one end where they sat to enjoy the fresh air and talk with visitors in the warm weather. The other end had an oilcloth-covered table with the water bucket, with dipper for drinking, and an icebox to keep food cool.

Other items sometimes kept on the back porch included nails for hanging extra pans used in the garden. There was usually a pile of wood ranked up on the far end of the porch out of the rain. The wood was cut the season before while it was green and placed in the dry to cure. Each piece was cut the proper length for the cook stove and ranked by type of wood for different cooking purposes.

My mom had a couple of old cabinets with drawers on our back porch. In it, she kept tools, screws, nails, along with her tiny oil

Great Uncle Joe Morris (left) and Curry Lam enjoy a visit on one end of Uncle Joe's front porch. The slop bucket for the hogs sat to the right of Uncle Joe. Uncle Joe's hog pen was across the road from the front porch and the kitchen was just inside the window behind Uncle Joe and Curry. (Picture courtesy of Mrs. Mary Turner, Joe and Millie Morris' daughter).

Great Aunt Millie is leaving the porch to collect seeds from her ancient hollyhocks. She loved to share her seeds with anyone who came to visit. Behind her, we can see the things one would find a "back" porch. (Picture courtesy of Mrs. Mary Turner, Joe and Millie Morris' daughter).

can used for keeping her sewing machine in good running order. The smell that came from that drawer when it was opened was a mixture of metal and oil. I always found that smell very inviting and enjoyed opening the tool drawer. You could find any version of poison that you wanted under the cabinets on Mom's porch. One very important item was located somewhere on the back porch–the fly sprayer and the DDT that was used to fight the houseflies that plagued the mountain home. Other items included garden dust with skull and crossbones, lye, medicines to drench the cows, calf bottles and nipples, half-filled oilcans, Lysol for the slop jar, and sharp syringes for medicating hogs, chickens, and cows. After several emergency trips to the doctor for stomach pumping, we discovered that most of these items had to be moved when the grandchildren arrived on earth.

Inside the House

Most Appalachian Mountain homes had some common features that reflected their survival cultures. Before electric lines reached the mountain hollows, homes were lit with kerosene lanterns. Kerosene was considered expensive and not easy to get because stores that sold it were few and far between. Therefore, folks in my grandparent's generation went to bed early–shortly after dark–and arose with sunrise in an effort to conserve kerosene. After electricity arrived in the mountains, each room in the house had one bare light bulb in the center of the ceiling with a string hanging down to turn the light on and off. At night when you needed to turn on a light, you stuck your hand out and walked toward the center of the room hoping to grab onto the light string. Most of the light strings were too short for children to reach them in fear that they would have a little fun by turning the lights on and off. The short light string made it very difficult for a child to maneuver into all the rooms in the house without a parent's permission and help in reaching the light string–very frustrating.

The ceiling light bulb offered great difficulties when you had to get up in the night to use the chamber pot. Some creative children, self included, tied a string to the end of the ceiling light string and attached it to a nail hammered into the wall just above the headboard on the bed. One simple wave of the hand in the dark located the string and there was light to see the path to the pot.

The Kitchen. The kitchen was usually the first room you entered as you went into the house from the back porch. The kitchen stove was located on the far end of the room on an outer wall. The stovepipe came up from the back of the stove and then turned into ninety-degree angle and went through the wall. Outside the house, the pipe turned upward into another ninety-degree angle. The stovepipe extended upward until it passed the edge of the roof. The turns in the pipe prevented the wind from shooting directly down the pipe and into the stove thus causing the fire to burn too fast and too "cold." A fast fire did not allow enough heat to build up in the stove to cook food or bake pies, cakes, and bread. There was also a damper in the straight section of pipe that came directly out of the stove. Mom knew exactly how to use the damper to control the heat in her stove. She knew by the sound of the fire if the damper needed adjusting. If she was busy peeling potatoes or making butter, she would ask me to turn the damper for her. She listened as the noises in the stove changed and told me when I had adjusted it the way she wanted it. I never understood the connection between the damper and the fire noises; and, unfortunately, Mom could not explain it. It was just something she learned over her many years of cooking.

The kitchen was always warm and filled with the lingering smells of the last meal along with the emerging smells of the upcoming meal. Cooking to feed the family never ended. Peggy, from Patrick County, described her mother's effort to feed ten children three meals a day. "She never stopped cooking," Peggy said. "All seasons of the year she had the wood stove hot and covered with pots and pans. It felt good in the winter and fall, but in the summer, the house was hot, and I will never forget the big sweat drops on Mama's face as she opened the oven to remove her delicious biscuits."

When breakfast was over and the dishes washed, preparation for dinner started. Once that meal was completed, pots of pinto or green beans or perhaps a ham bone for potpie were placed over the fire for supper.

The Living Room

When talking about my mountain home to my friends, I often spoke of the dining room where Dad spent his final years sitting at the end of the table playing solitaire for most of the day. Mom delivered his meals to him three times a day. He would interrupt his game, pick up the cards, eat, move the empty plate aside for Mom to pick up, and immediately resume his card game. I spoke of the kitchen where Mom cooked her wonderful meals and processed the food from the garden. I probably talked about the bedrooms in some context or another. Curiously, the mention of these rooms did not bring forth any response from my audience; however, when I mentioned the "living room," I was often asked, "What is the 'living room'? We had a 'parlor'." Is that what you mean by 'living' room?" I learned along the way that the parlor was very formal and the "living room" was very informal. The parlor was where the family did not live, and the living room was where the family did live.

For many years, the question, "What is a living room?" puzzled me. I wondered why someone would ask what a living room was as it was certainly an important room in my home, and all the mountain people that I knew used the term "living room." My answer to my friends was, "That's where we did most of our living, I guess."

The living room was a necessary space for family life cycle events for several reasons. The family was responsible for carrying out the major duties for survival–birthing and caring for the sick and dying. Hospitals or clinics were far away in distant cities and towns. Roads were few and those that existed were sometimes passable only when the weather was cooperating. Just one generation ago, a community may have had only one car and a generous owner available to drive sick folks to a doctor or a hospital.

The "living room" became the location for family life events because homes did not have central heat. They were heated with fireplaces and later stoves that were placed in only certain parts of the house. One stove was located in the kitchen for cooking the meals. A second stove provided heat in the living room just off the kitchen where the family spent a lot of their time between meals. The living room was the warmest room in the house. The fire in the living room stove was maintained twenty-four hours a day.

At least in my paternal grandparent's home, there was a lot of anxiety about keeping the fire burning in the living room. My dad would often ask Grandpa Austin and Grandma Molly to go for a ride with us on Sunday afternoons. They always refused to go together. Sometimes Grandma Molly would ride along with us to explore the mountain roads between Hopkins Gap and West Virginia. However, most of the time Grandma Molly stayed at home because, as she said, "I can't leave the house by itself." After some further questions, she admitted, "I am afraid the fire will go out." On the hottest days of the year, the living room stove was kept hot. The only difference was that Grandpa Austin moved his rocking chair a little further away from the summer fire to the point where he often missed the spittoon when he squirted tobacco juice toward where it sat near the living room stove. Thus, my answer to my friends who asked, "What is a living room?" was accurate when I said, "That's where we did most of our living."

Therefore, just like everything else in mountain culture, each room, and the porches, had distinct and utilitarian purposes.

However, the central location for family life cycle events–conception, birth, healing, and death–occurred in the living room where the "living room" bed allowed warmth from the fire, access to family caregivers, and visits from friends and neighbors.

PART I:

ARRIVING ON EARTH

Mountain life was about continuity from generation to generation. Houses passed from one generation to another because as children grew old enough for marriage, they stepped into the same roles as their grandfather and grandmother and father and mother before them. When it was time for a new baby to arrive, the mother-to-be knew where the birth would occur. Often it was in the same "living room" bed that she had been born in some years before; and, perhaps, the same bed that her mother or father had been born in.

Married couples expected to have large numbers of children. Women began having children as soon as they were married. If they did not die from complications of childbirth, birthing continued until the "change of life" or menopause. Breastfeeding was the main form of birth control, but it did not work for some women. Children numbered into the teens in many families, and a couple who had no children, or just one or two children, bore the brunt of nasty gossip.

Because of patriarchal family life, fathers and mothers preferred that a male child be born first. However, both genders assisted with the rigors of mountain life. Fathers and mothers often let a first-born female know that she was not their first choice. As a not-so-subtle way of letting her know, they told her what her name would have been if she were a boy. She often heard,

"We didn't even have a girl's name picked out." For example, my mother told me, "We had picked William for our first boy; when you came along, we didn't have a name. I got your name from the funeral director's wife."

Gender mattered when it came to welcoming a baby when it arrived in the "living room" bed. It dictated where that child could play, the explanation of its life from the perspective of religion, how it would wear its hair, how it dressed, and, finally, when it could eat at the Sunday dinner table.

A child born in the "living room" bed was most likely one of many children born to its mother. Usually a mother had her children very close to each other. In these cases, there was limited time to bond with a child before the next baby appeared in the "living room" bed, and the older children were often jealous of the new baby because it received all of the mother's attention.

Where a child fell in the birth order had significant consequences for the remainder of his or her life. The oldest child always had the benefits of being first but had to help care for the younger children. The middle child felt insecure and either withdrew or acted out for attention. The youngest child (often a "change-of-life" baby) was able to bond with the mother longer because the birth of this child ended the mother's childbearing years. Within the family, older siblings called a "change-of-life" baby derogatory names such as "spoiled brat" or "Momma's pet." The community labeled a "change-of-life" baby as "spoiled" and expected it to cause problems for the parents and the neighbors.

Being one of many children in the family also meant that a child was one of many in the extended family and the community. Therefore, children were born into a large social network of siblings, cousins, aunts, and uncles. In any case, being one of many exposed children to a wide variety of memorable characters.

In summary, in the Appalachian Mountains, most children arrived on earth in the "living room" bed. While the "living room" bed did not shape a child's future, it was the launching pad for a boy child's or girl child's future life where gender and birth order mattered. Being one of many placed a child in a large family setting with numerous aunts, uncles, and cousins with both positive and negative consequences.

Chapter 1

Being Born

"A baby is an angel whose wings decrease as his legs increase."
Anonymous

Up until the 1940's, most children in the rural Appalachian Mountains were born at home in the "living room" bed. Being born was a difficult and sometimes dangerous experience for the baby as well as its mother. Old headstones in the cemeteries attest to the fact that too often both the mother and child died and rested in the same grave. A wood fire in a stove or fireplace warmed the living room. A midwife attended the births, along with other female family members and female neighbors who came for support and assistance.

A mountain wife expected to deliver many children; therefore, it was common to try to determine how many children a woman would bear. There were many ways to do this; however, some determinations had to occur just after the birth of a new baby and while the mother lay in the "living room" bed. Just after the birth occurred, the midwife counted the number of lumps in the umbilical cord to determine how many more babies this mother would bear.

While the mother lay in the "living room" bed recovering from childbirth, her sisters and female friends jokingly used other methods to determine how many more children she would have. The new mother raised her eyebrows while her female companions counted the numbers of wrinkles in her forehead. That was the number of children she would bear. The new mother squeezed her hand into a fist and her friends counted the number of small lines between the two larger ones on the "pinky" side of her hand. The number of wrinkles equaled the number of children the woman would bear.

Since the typical mountain mother gave birth to between five and eight children, her lifetime chances of dying in childbirth ran as high as one in eight. This meant that if a woman had eight female friends or eight sisters, it was likely that one might die in childbirth. Death in childbirth was sufficiently common that many women regarded pregnancy with fear and dread.

◆◆◆◆◆◆◆◆◆◆◆◆◆◆◆◆◆◆◆◆◆◆◆◆◆◆◆◆◆◆◆◆◆◆

Childbed Fever . . .

Occasionally a new mother would become very ill three or four days after the birth of her baby. Her symptoms included high fever and sweats. In the first half of the twentieth century, childbed fever was the single most common cause of maternal deaths, accounting for about half of all deaths related to childbirth, and was second only to tuberculosis in killing women of childbearing age. The disease was contagious and caused by strep infection. Childbed fever spread with midwives and doctors as they went from one birth to the next without changing clothing or thoroughly cleaning their hands.

Prior to the twentieth century, one obstetrician dissected the corpse of a woman who died of childbed fever. He put her uterus in his coat pocket so that he could show it to his students. He felt neither gloves nor hand washing was necessary. "The same evening," he wrote, "without changing my clothes, I attended the delivery of a poor woman in the community; she died. Next morning I went with the same clothes to assist . . . with a woman . . . , whom I delivered with forceps; she died." His language is a reminder that no one in those times spoke of delivering a baby. Doctors and midwives talked of delivering women from the peril of childbirth. (1)

◆◆◆◆◆◆◆◆◆◆◆◆◆◆◆◆◆◆◆◆◆◆◆◆◆◆◆◆◆◆◆◆◆◆

In addition to her anxieties about pregnancy, an expectant mother was always concerned about the death of her young child. The death of a child in infancy was very common. In the harsher living conditions in the Appalachian Mountains, three children in ten died before reaching the age of ten.

◆◆◆◆◆◆◆◆◆◆◆◆◆◆◆◆◆◆◆◆◆◆◆◆◆◆◆◆◆◆◆◆◆◆

"Second Summer" Sickness . . .

In the past, "second summer" sickness was a term used to explain the deaths of some children as they entered the second summer of their lives. The symptoms included severe stomach cramps and diarrheic, bloody excrement. Some folks called this same condition "bloody flux." "Second summer" sickness or "bloody flux" occurred around the time the mother switched her child from breast milk to cow's milk as the main source of food. Without alternative foods such as infant formula, and without education, most mothers did not recognize the possible role of cow's milk as the cause of their child's discomfort and often death.

In my family, we called the condition "bloody flux." We believed that feeding a young child a strawberry caused it. My mother told stories about some children in Hopkins Gap who screamed and strained from the cramps of bloody flux and ultimately died. Today we know that many children are allergic to cows' milk, and we have infant formula to use after weaning from the breast. (2)

◆◆◆◆◆◆◆◆◆◆◆◆◆◆◆◆◆◆◆◆◆◆◆◆◆◆◆◆◆◆◆◆◆◆

Birth certificates of children in the Appalachian Mountains often noted the number of children that had been born to a mother along with the number of stillborn babies and those who died in early childhood. My Uncle Richard Morris was born in Hopkins Gap in 1926. He was the last born of Grandma Mary Morris' eighteen children. Richard's birth certificate shows (see center right of the birth certificate) that Grandma Mary had already lost five of her eighteen children in infancy or early childhood. One baby was stillborn. As noted on lower left side of the birth certificate, Grandma Mary died on September 16, 1926, just four months after Richard's birth. She was thirty-nine years old.

Given these facts, it is not surprising that many superstitions surrounded pregnancy and childbirth. It was widely believed that a mother might disfigure her unborn child if she looked upon a horrible event or heard a sudden loud noise. For example, if a rabbit ran across her path or jumped out in front of a pregnant woman,

PLACE OF BIRTH
COUNTY OF Rockingham
MAGISTERIAL DISTRICT OF Plains
OR
INC. TOWN OF
OR
CITY OF

CERTIFICATE OF BIRTH
COMMONWEALTH OF VIRGINIA
BUREAU OF VITAL STATISTICS
STATE BOARD OF HEALTH

22573

REGISTRATION DISTRICT NO. 824C REGISTERED NO. 19 (FOR USE OF LOCAL REGISTRAR)
NO. ST., WARD
(If birth occurs in a hospital or other institution, give name of same instead of street and number)

FULL NAME OF CHILD Richard Eugene Morris
(Do not write in this space if child is not yet named; make supplemental report as directed)

BOY OR GIRL? boy | To be answered ONLY in event of plural births | 4 Twin, triplet or other | 5 Number, in order of birth | 6 ARE PARENTS MARRIED? yes | 7 DATE OF BIRTH May 25 1926 (Name of Month) (Day) (Year)

FATHER
FULL NAME John Wesley Morris
PRESENT ADDRESS (Usual place of abode) (If nonresident, give place and State) Harrisonburg R.F.D. 7
WHITE OR COLORED? white
11 AGE AT LAST BIRTHDAY 44 (Years)
BIRTHPLACE (city or place) (State or country) Virginia
OCCUPATION Nature of Industry Labor
DID YOU USE THE DROPS IN THE BABY'S EYES? yes
IF NOT, TELL WHY

MOTHER
16 FULL NAME BEFORE MARRIAGE Mary Ellen Lame
17 PRESENT ADDRESS (Usual place of abode) (If nonresident, give place and State) Harrisonburg R.F.D. #7
18 WHITE OR COLORED? white
19 AGE AT LAST BIRTHDAY 39 (Years)
20 BIRTHPLACE (city or place) (State or country) Virginia
21 OCCUPATION Nature of Industry at home
22 INCLUDING THIS CHILD
Number of children of this Mother now living 12
Number of children of this Mother born alive and now dead 5
Number of children of this Mother stillborn 1

CERTIFICATE OF ATTENDING PHYSICIAN OR MIDWIFE*
23 I HEREBY CERTIFY THAT I ATTENDED THE BIRTH OF THIS CHILD, WHO WAS born alive (Born Alive or Stillborn) AT 1:45 A. M. (Hour A. M. or P. M.) ON THE DATE ABOVE STATED.

*When there was no attending physician or midwife then the father, householder, etc., should make this return. If a child breathes even once, it must not be reported as stillborn.

24 (SIGNATURE) F. A. Stoutamire M.D.
25 STATE WHETHER PHYSICIAN OR MIDWIFE Physician
26 ADDRESS OF PHYSICIAN OR MIDWIFE Broadway Va
27 WITNESS
(Signature of Witness necessary only when question 24 is signed by mark)

30 ADDITIONAL INFORMATION ADDED FROM A SUPPLEMENTAL REPORT FROM
Mother died 9/16 26
REGISTRAR

28 FILED June 8 1926 (Date Received by Registrar)
29 J. W. Pickering LOCAL REGISTRAR

her unborn child might have a harelip. Another belief stated that if a pregnancy woman looked at the moon, her child might become a lunatic or sleepwalker.

My mother told me a story about a crippled girl whose last name was McDorman. She came to church at Gospel Hill Mennonite Church in Hopkins Gap. Her body froze in a position with her knees pulled up toward her body, and her elbows bent toward her upper arms. Her brother pulled her in a little red wagon. I often saw them come up the aisle of the church. Of course, I asked Mom what had happened to the girl.

Mom told me, "Her daddy liked to catch rabbits and cut the tendons in their legs. Then he turned them loose and laughed as they tried to run and jump. His wife begged him to stop doing that to the rabbits or he would mark the baby she was carrying. He just laughed at her. When the baby was born, she had tendons in her legs and arms that were so tight she could not straighten them out. That's why she can't walk."

Societal superstitions placed many restrictions on the mother's behavior while she was pregnant. For example, many thought an expectant mother's ungratified food cravings could cause a mark to imprint on her child's body. The husband or other relatives made every effort to find any foods that the mother craved during her pregnancy. Mom told me about a woman in Hopkins Gap who had a very strong desire for beets during her pregnancy. She was not able to get any. The mother blamed the reddish colored birthmarks on her daughter's arm on her unsatisfied craving. She claimed the marks even looked like beets. "A lot of women marked their babies by craving strawberries. I've seen babies with strawberry birthmarks on the back of their neck," Mom said. Many pregnant women did not attend funerals because they feared that looking on a corpse would mark the baby. In addition, pregnant women were not to stoop or reach high because the umbilical cord would wrap itself around the baby's neck and cause its death.

Mom related a story about a monkey that jumped out in

front of her when she was walking on the street before I was born. The monkey was with a man who was playing an accordion for contributions. When Mom walked by, the monkey jumped at her. "I kicked the monkey away from me. Your daddy got mad at me and told me to behave myself. I told him that the monkey had probably marked you. I was scared to look at you when you were born. Thank God, you didn't look like a monkey," she said.

It was important for a woman to give her husband a son as the first-born. Therefore, folks devised many ways to determine if a pregnant woman was carrying a boy or a girl. For example, if you can tell a woman is pregnant by looking at her from the back, the child is a girl. If a pregnant woman carries her unborn child high and mostly in front, it will be a boy.

Another way to determine the sex of an unborn child was to thread a needle and pass it over the pregnant woman's wrist. If the needle moved in a circle, the baby would be a boy; if it moved back and forth in a straight line, the infant would be a girl. If the pregnant woman was carrying a girl and wanted a boy, some believed there was at least one way to change the sex. If a pregnant woman could kiss her own elbow, it would change the sex of her unborn child.

Because of the desire to birth sons, a lot of effort went into determining the sex of the next child prior to conception. Thus, a woman tried to get pregnant under a full moon, so the baby would be a boy. In addition, if a husband hung his trousers over the right bedpost at night before going to bed, his next child would be a son. A variation on this was for the man and wife to switch sides of the bed on which they slept in an effort to change the sex of the next baby to either a girl or a boy.

The "living room" bed, amidst the warmth of the living room stove, provided the atmosphere necessary for conceiving and birthing many babies. One baby had barely found his or her legs to walk before another one arrived to replace him or her. In my experience with aunts and uncles giving birth, every new baby brought pride and joy to its mom and dad.

Chapter 2

Mom's Babies

"Before you were conceived I wanted you
Before you were born I loved you
Before you were here an hour I would die for you
This is the miracle of life."

Maureen Hawkins

My birth and my siblings' births exemplify the way that many mountain children were born up until the early 1950's. When it was time for me to be born in 1941, many women in the mountains were still having their babies at home in the "living room" bed. However, my own birth occurred in Rockingham Memorial Hospital because, as Mom said, "I refused to be born like everybody else."

Mom started labor pains with me on a Monday. She sent my dad to Hopkins Gap to get the midwife, Nettie Conley, and Grandma Molly. As soon as he left, she completed some initial preparations. These included stoking the fire with wood; putting a pot of water on the stove to boil; laying out clothing for the new baby; and padding the "living room" bed to catch birthing fluids. When those tasks were finished, she lay down in the bed expecting that her first baby would be born soon.

Nettie and Grandma Molly arrived and stayed with Mom

until Wednesday evening while Nettie timed the labor pains and checked for dilation. Mom told me many times, "I just kept on having labor pains, but you just seemed to not want to be born. I guess you just didn't want to come out into the world."

After the third day of fruitless labor pains, Nettie told my Dad to call Dr. Charles Watson to come to the house and examine Mom. That was no easy task in the early 1940s. Dad had to drive to John I. Myers' house where the only phone in the community was located. He called the doctor who lived in Broadway, about twenty miles away as the crow flies. Dr. Watson had to travel all the way from Broadway to Mt. Clinton just across the mountain from Hopkins Gap. Today the trip takes about twenty minutes. In 1941, it was only a gravel road and just wide enough for two cars to cautiously pass each other. Cars did not travel very fast. Dr. Watson had patients to see all day before he could make a house call. He arrived at Mom's bedside sometime late on Thursday afternoon.

After the doctor's examination, he recommended that Dad call an ambulance the next morning and have Mom admitted to the hospital. The next day was Friday, May 9. The ambulance from McMullen's Funeral Home arrived around noon for the trip to the hospital. I was born that evening at 8:30.

I never did come out on my own, so Dr. Watson used forceps to pull me from the birth canal. I came onto this earth with two holes in my head. The skin on my neck was bloody, and my nose smashed to one side. Mom told me many times during my life, "I cried when I saw you. I thought you were scarred forever. God, you were ugly."

All my life, when I did something Mom didn't like, she would say, "You've been bull headed since before you come into this world." She never failed to follow this statement, once again, with the story of my birth. She would touch my forehead to let me know where the holes were, as she described, in detail, how I appeared immediately after my birth. The very descriptive story would have lasted a whole day if I had stood still and listened.

My brother, Larry, was born sixteen months after me. Of course, I was too young to remember his birth. Mom told me later that he was also born in the hospital because the midwife and Dr. Watson were scared to try his birth at home because of the problems she had with my birth. Larry was born without a problem. By the third pregnancy with my sister, Brenda, Mom was ready to try having her at home. Brenda was born in 1944, seventeen months after Larry, at home in the "living room" bed. Nettie Conley, the midwife, attended Brenda's birth, with assistance from Grandma Molly Shifflett and Aunt Goldie, Mom's sister. According to Mom, she had no problems with Brenda's birth. Six weeks after Brenda's birth, the U. S. Army drafted Dad. Brenda was fifteen months old when he returned from the war.

The first birth that I remember was that of my second brother, John, who was born at home in the "living room" bed in 1946. He was born eight-and-a-half months after Dad returned from fighting in World War II. The timing of his birth upset Mom. She thought everybody would think Dad was not John's father. Mom carefully explained many times during her life, "I was really big with John, and my big belly always put me off balance when I milked Ole Jerse. I kinda had to lean over and milk her instead of settin' on a stool. I was leaned over milkin' when a bee came into the barn and flew up to Ole Jerse's head. I guess it was after the molasses in her grain that she was eatin'. She jerked her head up, and I yelled at her, 'Stand still, Jerse.' About that time, the bee buzzed around her head again, and she whirled around and hit me in the stomach with her rear end. I felt the baby sorta jump inside my belly. I started having pains early the next morning. John was born two weeks early because of Ole Jerse; but, if I had carried him another two weeks, I don't know if I could'a had him. He already weighed ten-and-a-half pounds."

Preparing for the Birth

As soon as Mom discovered she was pregnant for the fourth time in five years, she started preparing for the birth. She already had many things stored in the attic that she needed for the new baby. Mom called diapers "*hippons.*" This word came from the Pennsylvania Dutch language that at least one family in Hopkins Gap used when I was a child. In those days, there was no such thing as store-bought, throwaway diapers. The soiled diapers were soaked in cold water with borax; washed in hot water and bleach; hung out on the clothesline to dry; ironed, folded and put away until needed again.

Mom sewed the diapers in three sizes: tiny for the newborn, medium for the six-to-twelve month old, and large for after one year until the child learned to use the pot. As her babies grew out of the tiny ones, she stored them in the attic. These had lasted through three infants and Mom simply needed to locate, wash, iron, and fold them again.

◆◆◆◆◆◆◆◆◆◆◆◆◆◆◆◆◆◆◆◆◆◆◆◆◆◆◆◆◆◆◆◆◆

Bird's Eye Cloth . . .

In the nineteenth and early twentieth centuries, women made diapers for their children from an absorbent cotton cloth called bird's eye, which had a pattern that looked like a bird's eye. The soiled diapers were soaked in a tub of cold water with borax and then washed in the old wringer washing machine. The soaking removed most stains and then hot washing water, with a bit of bleach, returned the cloth to pure white for the next use.

Because of the extent of absorbency of bird's eye cloth, many women made menstrual pads for themselves and their daughters from bird's eye cloth. Again, the soiled pads were soaked in cold water with borax to remove the bloodstains and then washed in hot water with bleach. In all seasons of the year, women poured the bloody water on the garden as fertilizer.

◆◆

Larry and I learned about the new baby in the attic of the old storehouse where we lived. Mom said, "I need to go to the attic to find something, and I want you all to go with me." The real reason for asking us to go with her was the fact that she knew we would be into some of our mean tricks if she left us downstairs alone.

Mom started to climb up the rickety stairs that hugged the kitchen wall. There was no handrail. She placed her right hand on the wall for support. I climbed up right behind her. Larry was just learning to climb stairs, so he got down on his hands and knees and came up behind us. We were both excited about a chance to get into the attic. I had been up there before and had recognized the abundance of junk, boxes, and old clothes to get into. It was dark and mysterious. The only natural light came in through a small window high above the kitchen door.

At the top of the stairs was a push-up door with hinges on one side. When Mom pushed up on the door, the dirt fell through the cracks into her face. The hinges creaked with age as the door fell back onto the attic floor, filling the air with a cloud of dust. She stepped up into the attic. The beam of light from the window displayed cobwebs and newly disturbed dust particles lingering in the air. Mom moved slowly toward the center of the attic as she warned us to watch our step. She turned and took Larry's hand so he would not step back and fall down the stairs. Mom reached up and pulled a dusty string attached to a ceiling light with just a naked bulb screwed into it. When she pulled the string, the attic flooded with light and revealed even more cobwebs and dust. Mom walked slowly toward a stack of boxes in the corner. She held Larry close to her leg as she opened a box and began to take out the tiny bird's eye diapers.

As Mom piled up the little diapers on another box nearby, she told us we were going to have another sister or brother. Larry was too young to understand that a new baby meant that he would be one of four instead of one of three. There was also the possibility that he would not be the only boy anymore. He seemed happy that a new baby was on the way.

I, on the other hand, had already felt the hurt of being one of three, and had often thought about how nice it would be to be an only child. The arrival of this new baby meant that I definitely was only one of many, and all my cuteness and "first baby" stuff that had happened and had been forgotten long ago anyhow, would now be totally lost in the excitement of this new baby.

Occasionally Mom told me that I had the prettiest blue eyes in the world and that people had stopped her on the streets of Harrisonburg to tell her how pretty my eyes were. She had bought me a sky-blue snowsuit that she said, "Really made your blue eyes stand out." The occasions when she told me about my blue eyes had grown fewer and farther between. Now, I would never hear the "blue eyes" story again. Oh God, what if the new baby was another boy? I had definitely felt the sting of my mother's disappointment in me for being a first-born female.

The situation did not get any better, when Mom said, "Now, Peggy, since you are the oldest, you will have to help me with this new baby." I knew she meant exactly what she was saying because I had already been helping with Larry and Brenda. Thinking back on that moment when I heard that another baby was coming, I must have had mixed feeling of pride, joy, dread, fear, and just plain jealousy.

Over the next six months, Mom stayed busy getting ready for the birth. She sewed for hours at a time. My cousin, Joyce, spent a lot of time at our house. "What are you making?" she asked Mom.

"I'm sewing doll baby clothes," Mom answered. She picked a drawer in the living room dresser and put the new little baby outfits that she sewed or bought in it. Mom often opened the drawer. She lovingly rubbed her hands over the little soft gowns and newly washed bird's eye diapers.

I peeped in the drawer every time I saw her open it. The smell of baby lotion and powder filled my nostrils and made me as anxious as she was for the new baby to arrive. She showed me a few little gowns that I had worn when I was a newborn. One corner of the drawer bulged with under shirts and bands for the baby's belly. There was a spot for Johnson's baby oil and powder and a little box of diaper pins with little plastic duck heads on them. These diaper pins were the first ones I had seen with duck heads on them. In my few years on this earth, I had watched many babies get clean diapers because the women in Hopkins Gap were having babies all the time. We were always around Uncle Shirley and Aunt Ethel, and they were on their fourth baby. I asked about the duck head pins. Mom told me, "Well they are kinda pretty, and I guess they keep the metal pins from rubbing against the baby's skin."

Mom was always talking about the new baby. I heard her talking with Dad about what she wanted to name the baby if it was a boy or a girl. They talked it over and agreed that if it were a boy, they would name it after Mom's father, John Wesley Morris. If it were a girl, they would name it after Dad's mother, Molly Frances Shifflett. Dad wanted his middle name used with "John" so the baby's name, if it was a boy, was going to be John McCaril. Mom didn't like "McCaril" so she suggested they use "Carroll" instead. Dad agreed.

"It's fine with me to use your middle name, but I wouldn't name a dog "Molly Beatrice,'" Mom told Dad. Her middle name was Beatrice, and she hated it until the day she died. After I grew up, I teased Mom by calling her Beatrice, but always kept a good distance from her quick hand, because it would have landed across my mouth before I could blink an eye. Mom and Dad planned to have the baby at home with the help of Nettie Conley, Dr. Watson, Aunt Goldie, and Grandma Molly. All of them had been present at the birth of Brenda just a year and a half before.

Finally, with the help of Mom's cow, Ole Jerse, the labor pains started before dawn on April 18, 1946. I heard Mom and Dad get out of bed. They were hustling around and talking in whispers. Mom came into the bedroom and told me, "You need to get up and help with Larry and Brenda. The new baby is coming today. Daddy will take you all with him to Aunt Goldie's house. You all are gonna stay with her while I have the baby."

In those days, preparation had to begin immediately when the labor pains started because of the length of time it took to get the midwife, the doctor, and any female assistants to the home for the birth. Dad rushed around and hustled us into the car. I was scared to leave Mom behind by herself, but I assume that she made final preparations until the labor pains got harder and were coming close together. Then she lay down in the "living room" bed and waited for the arrival of the midwife and the doctor.

Dad drove the car on past Aunt Goldie's house. I asked him why he did not stop. He said, "You all can ride with me to the Gap to get Net Conley. I'll drop you off on the way back home." Dad drove fast across Little North Mountain and down through Hopkins Gap. We liked it when he drove fast and swerved around the turns. We flopped around in the back seat and giggled. He stopped the car in front of Nettie's house and went in to tell her Mom was in labor. He came back to the car and waited with us while Nettie gathered the essential birthing equipment that she carried in her black bag. I rolled across the front seat and sat next to him while we waited.

In a few minutes, Nettie came trudging down the bank from her house to the road. She had a huge grin on her face. I rolled over the front seat of the car again and sat in the back with Larry and Brenda. Nettie slid into the passenger seat holding her black bag, which contained silver nitrate and a disinfectant for the mother's external area and Nettie's hands. Silver nitrate was a liquid disinfectant dropped in the new baby's eyes to prevent the transmission of sexually transmitted diseases from their mothers. Nettie placed the black bag on the seat between Dad and her. She immediately began asking Dad about how far apart the birthing pains were when he left. He answered her questions as we crossed Little North Mountain.

Dad stopped at Aunt Goldie's house, and she welcomed us into her living room. She got in the car with Dad and Nettie, and we stayed with her oldest daughter, Ruby, as we waited for the news about our baby brother or sister. Dad drove Nettie and Aunt Goldie across the hill to our house. In a few minutes, we saw him drive fast past Aunt Goldie's house. We learned later that Dad was going to John I. Myers' house to call Dr. Watson. After Dad called Dr. Watson, he went back across the mountain to Hopkins Gap and picked up Grandma Molly.

Finally, Dad came back to Aunt Goldie's to wait for the new baby. Men stayed out of the living room while women gave birth. Once when I asked Mom why men could not be in the room when the baby was born, I got some story about how it was bad luck for a man to look upon his wife's private parts while a baby was being born. When I was older, that belief made no sense to me since he was looking upon her private parts when she got pregnant in the first place.

By the time my youngest brother was born in 1952, we had moved just over the hill to live in Aunt Goldie's house. Aunt Goldie had moved her "living room" bed to a back room away from the fire. Times had changed a lot, and Mom agreed to go to the hospital for the birth. Dad came home and announced that we had a baby brother. Without seeing him or touching him, we immediately loved the tiny addition to our household.

Chapter 3

Midwives of Hopkins Gap

"We don't accomplish anything in this world alone . . . and whatever happens is the result of the whole tapestry of one's life and all the weavings of individual threads from one to another that creates something."

Sandra Day O'Connor

Nettie Conley was perhaps the last of many midwives who served the women of Hopkins Gap and surrounding areas. I do not recall her helping with any births after my brother John was born in 1946. From a search of birth certificates between 1912 and 1917, Pat Ritchie and other researchers discovered ten women who helped with the births of more than thirty children born in Hopkins Gap. (3) Many births before and after 1912 were not officially

This is a picture of Nettie Conley, the midwife who delivered my sister, Brenda, and my brother, John. Nettie poses here with a small number of the children she delivered in Hopkins Gap. Pictured with Nettie are Rainey Conley, Buck Crawford, Sherman Conley, Leroy Conley, Irene Conley, Doris Crawford, Honey Crawford, Betty Lou Crawford, and Mary Ann Crawford. (Photo courtesy of Kenneth (Bunson) Morris).

recorded, so the thirty babies delivered by midwives were probably just a small sample of the births in Hopkins Gap that midwives attended.

I have found no indication that any of the midwives that birthed babies all along the Appalachian range had formal training. Most of the women I talked to said that the knowledge of midwifery came from observation and listening to older midwives. My mother illustrated this fact when Aunt Ethel went into labor with her second baby, Betty. Uncle Shirley drove Aunt Ethel to our house where Mom made her comfortable in the "living room" bed. In a short while, Betty was born with Mom serving as the midwife. Mom had already had three babies, but she had not been an observing or practicing midwife.

Mary Morris, my maternal grandmother, was one midwife mentioned in the Ritchie research. In 1917, she assisted with the births of Irene Conley, Luther Arlis Kirkpatrick, and Mary Virginia Morris, my cousin. In 1919, Mary Morris, my Mom's

CERTIFICATE OF BIRTH
COMMONWEALTH OF VIRGINIA
Bureau of Vital Statistics
State Board of Health

File No.—For State Registrar Only. 12260

1 PLACE OF BIRTH
County of Rockingham
Magisterial District of Linville
or Inc. Town of ______ Registration District No. 829 Registered No. 7 (For use of Local Registrar)
or City of Dalas (No. ______ St.; ______ Ward)
(If birth occurs in a hospital or other institution, give name of same instead of street and number)

2 Full Name of Child Norman McCaril Shifflett
(Do not write in this space if child is not yet named; make supplemental report as directed.)

3 Boy or Girl? Boy | 4 Twin or Triplet? | 5 Number, in order of birth (To be answered only in event of Twins or Triplets) | 6 Are Parents Married? Yes | 7 Date of Birth March 9, 1919 (Name of Month) (Day) (Year)

FATHER
8 Full Name John A. Shifflett
9 Present Address of Father Dalas Va.
10 White or Colored White
11 Age at Last Birthday 40 (Years)
12 Birthplace Green Co. Va.
13 Occupation Farmer
20 Number of children born to this mother, including present birth Eight

MOTHER
14 Full Name Before Marriage Mollie F. Crawford
15 Present Address of Mother Dalas Va.
16 White or Colored White
17 Age at Last Birthday 34 (Years)
18 Birthplace Rockingham Co. Va.
19 Occupation House keeper
21 Number of children of this mother now living, including present birth Eight

CERTIFICATE OF ATTENDING PHYSICIAN OR MIDWIFE*
22 I hereby certify that I attended the birth of this child, who was born alive (Born Alive or Stillborn) at 9-20 P. M. (Hour A. M. or P. M.) on the date above stated.

23 (Signature) Mary E. Morris
24 State whether Physician or Midwife Midwife
25 Address of Physician or Midwife Dalas, Va.
26 Witness ______ (Signature of Witness necessary only when question 23 is signed by mark)
27 Filed March 1919 (Date received by Registrar) 28 J. C. Cooper Local Registrar.

Additional information as to questions ______ added from a supplemental report.
______ 191__
______ Registrar.

mother, assisted with the birth of my father in 1919 as indicated on the birth certificate shown here.

My Grandma Mary was about to become pregnant with her fourteenth child–my mother–when she was a midwife to my Grandma Molly for the birth of my dad. The fact that my mother assisted Aunt Ethel and Grandma Mary Morris helped bring my dad into the world, is a testimony to the interdependence of women in Hopkins Gap, an isolated community in the Allegheny Mountains.

Midwife Duties

There was little or no change in the duties of the midwife from the time of the first written record to the work of the Hopkins Gap midwives. The midwife coached the mother through her labor, encouraging her to breathe and to push at the right moment so the baby moved through the birth canal. If a problem occurred, the midwife put her hand inside the mother, turned the baby in the right direction, or moved an arm or leg into the correct position.

Another sad duty of the midwife was to arrange for the disposal of the bodies of stillborn children. Babies born dead were called "blue babies." This was a lay term used before the knowledge that "blue babies" died from congenital heart problems. Other babies were simply born dead. A possible cause was the Rh factor in the mother's blood. If the mother was Rh negative and the fetus was Rh positive, the mother's body responded to the positive Rh by making antibodies that attacked the fetus. In severe cases, the mother's antibodies caused stillbirth.

A stillbirth occurred with little or no ceremony. The midwife called the father to the "living room" bed and told him that the baby was dead. She instructed him to go outside in the far end of the back yard and dig a small grave. She then wrapped the baby in a cloth and laid it in the grave. The father filled in the grave. These little graves were not marked and the baby received no name. All along the Appalachian Mountains, folks talked about stillbirth and described a similar process for burying the baby.

Hopkins Gap folks still tell a poignant story about stillborn babies. "Cry Baby Lane" is an unofficial name for a road to an old homestead. According to the story, a mother who lived there birthed eight "blue babies." The midwife and father buried them in the fashion described above. The new owner of that homestead is Dr. Tim Carter, a friend and professor at James Madison University. He asked me about the unofficial name to his homestead as he was considering the purchase of this property. Recently, he invited me to his home. He showed me a spot in the corner of the yard where colorful crocuses faithfully appear every spring. We wondered if this corner of the yard served as a burial spot for the stillborn babies. Whether it did or not, Tim has treated the area as sacred.

Nettie Conley carried out her midwife duties with expertise and grace. According to Aunt Ethel, "Net had a steady hand and nothing scared her. If a baby wasn't turned in the right way, she just went inside and turned it around." She added, "Net loved her work. You could tell because she grinned the whole time that the baby was coming out. She helped me with my first babies, and when the pains got hard, I would yell out 'I can't stand to do this,' and Net would say, 'Just think of all the women who have done this before you. Push harder.' What she said helped me get through it. Net was a lot of fun anytime I was around her."

My cousin, Joyce, said, "I remember Net was a lot of fun especially if she had a little 'nip' of moonshine. She loved to dance. My favorite memory of her was one time when she came to our house. My daddy was playing music and everybody was passin' a pint around. Net danced all over the house with me."

When Nettie arrived at our house on April 18, 1946, she found Mom lying in the "living room" bed. She checked the time between birth pains and the amount of dilation. After she was satisfied that all was moving along fine, she went outside to the wood yard, found the ax, and brought it into the house through the living room door. She knelt down on her knees and pushed the ax under the living room bed where Mom was lying. She said, "There now, that will help to 'cut' the pain."

When Mom's fourth baby arrived that day, Nettie announced, "You have a big baby boy," as she checked for mucous in his throat and gently whacked him to make him cry. Then she immediately placed the baby to Mom's breast for the first feeding. According to Mom, Nettie kept a close watch to make sure the new baby was receiving milk. She checked the baby's lower lip to see if it was blocking access to the nipple and made sure that he had positioned his tongue correctly under the nipple to allow the sucking motion. After Nettie noted that the baby was sucking properly, she turned to the business of cutting the umbilical cord.

When Mom was telling me this story, I asked her, "What was Dr. Watson doing all this time?"

"He was just watching and telling Nettie what a good job she was doing. He wouldn't have been there at all if I hadn't had so much trouble having you," she replied.

Nettie was following tradition when she placed the baby to the breast before she cut the umbilical cord. She knew from many years of birthing that normal bleeding associated with childbirth slowed as soon as the baby began to nurse. Contemporary breastfeeding experts know, through research and observation, that as soon as the new baby begins to suckle the mother's breast, the uterus begins to shrink back into place, and the bleeding associated with childbirth decreases; thus, there is less chance of hemorrhaging. Suckling releases the hormone *prolactin*, known as the "mothering hormone." It functions to bond the mother and baby to each other. Breastfeeding experts today believe *prolactin* is basic to the survival of the human race because without the bonding effects of this hormone, the mother might have walked away from the wiggly, screaming, and demanding little brat she had just released into the world (4).

Mom had no problem with breastfeeding the new baby

because he was the fourth child she had breastfed. Most women in the rural Appalachian Mountains breastfed their babies, or at least tried to breastfeed, because they had grown up watching other women breastfeed (their moms, aunts, neighbors); thus, it came to them more naturally.

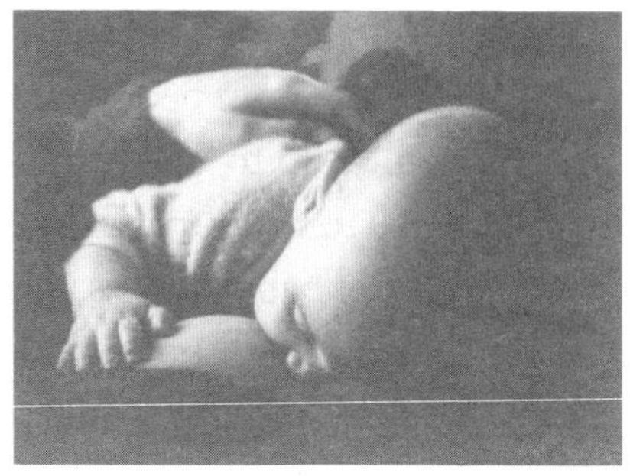

Scottie Pritchard of Grayson County, Virginia, as she nurses one of her four children.

Anti-breast feeding commercialism and brainwashing, which occurred during the 1940s and 1950s, did not reach mountain mothers partially because of isolation from the outside world. It was the daughters of Mom's generation, or my own generation, who bought into the anti-breastfeeding movement in the United State. Widespread advertising of infant formula and the view that women's breasts were objects of beauty for men instead of the "natural" and preferred way to feed babies brought on this movement. These "city" ways reached the mountains by radio and ultimately television. Now women are taught how to breast feed.

Nettie's next duty was to clean the baby. She used warm water and mild soap to clear the birthing substances. After he was clean, Nettie massaged his body with baby oil and began the process of dressing him for the first time. The first item of clothing was the "bellyband." All babies wore bands around their stomach for the first six weeks of their life. The band was a long, narrow rectangular cloth made of several layers of cotton. It was about four inches wide. The bellyband held the baby's navel tightly so it would not rupture. Nettie laid a bellyband on the bed and turned the baby on its stomach on top of the band. She took the two ends of the band and pulled them tight together in the middle of the baby's back. The baby screamed with pain as she pinned the band in place.

After Mom took over the care of the new baby, I watched

her put the bellyband on him. Mom told me, "The belly where the navel cord comes off is a weak place and lots of babies, when they cry real hard, get a rupture right around their navel. The band holds the belly really right until the weak spot can heal and get strong." When she was getting ready to put the band on the baby, she got her roll of surgical tape and tore off two or three short pieces. She stuck the ends onto the edge of a dresser until she needed them. She took the fingers on her left hand and gently massaged until she could push the navel back into the belly. Then she used the fingers on her right hand and pinched up the flesh on either side of the baby's navel so that it covered the belly button. With her freed-up left hand, she took the pieces of tape and taped the pinched up belly skin so that the navel was held snugly back in the baby's belly.

◆ ◆

Belly Button Repair Woman . . .

The use of a navel band stopped in my generation of women and some babies ended up with navel hernias at around six weeks of age. Mom was the hernia-repair person in Hopkins Gap. For many years, mothers brought their babies to Mom. She fussed at them for not using a navel band, and then she went to the drawer for her surgical tape and performed her form of surgery on the bulging belly button. "You know you should've used a band when this baby was first born," Mom scolded the mother. "I might be able to fix the rupture, but you'll have to keep a band on this baby for a while. You bring him [or her] back to me in four weeks, and I will take the tape off and see if it has growed back in place. If it's not healed, you will have to take it to the hospital, and they'll fix the rupture with surgery."

The mother watched Mom perform the massage to locate the hernia, push the belly button back into the belly, squeeze the skin over it, and tape it. The baby always screamed as loud and hard as it could. The mother stood by and watched with a lot of sympathetic pain on her face as her baby screamed. When the procedure was over, Mom placed a band on the belly, and the baby usually quieted down immediately. Mom would scold the mother again. "You see, now he [or she] feels more secure. Every time he [or she] cried, that rupture pushed out and got bigger. You should have used a band in the first place, and this would not have happened," she would say.

I remember only one occasion when Mom checked the baby's belly some weeks later and found the hernia had not healed. She explained to the mother, "You waited too long to have me to work on it." All other times, the baby's belly was just as smooth as it could be after the taping and wearing the band. Mom glowed with pride as she showed the mother the results of her work, "Now ain't that better than putting your baby in the hospital to have this done. I didn't have to cut a thing–no scar and a beautiful belly button–and it didn't cost you a cent." As time went by, mothers forgot that Mom could repair their babies' belly button hernias, and the hospital got all the business.

◆◆◆◆◆◆◆◆◆◆◆◆◆◆◆◆◆◆◆◆◆◆◆◆◆◆◆◆◆◆◆◆◆

The next piece of clothing for the new baby was a tiny bird's eye diaper, followed by an undershirt, soft gown, and a little flannel blanket. Once Nettie dressed the baby and wrapped him in a blanket, she asked Grandma Molly to bring her a chair from the kitchen. Nettie and most folks believed that a new baby should be carried upstairs soon after it was born, so that it would "go up in the world," as an adult. The house we lived in did not have an upstairs other than the attic, so Nettie held the baby tight to her chest and stepped up on the chair so that the new baby would "go up in the world." After the ritual, Nettie laid the new baby in Mom's arms as she lay in the "living room" bed. Mom placed him against her bulging breast for the second feeding.

Later on Mom said to me, "Nettie told me to keep the baby in bed with me and to let him nurse whenever he wanted. I could always tell when my babies were getting hungry by the way they started wiggling their arms and legs. I would just roll over on my side and let them get to the nipple. Nettie said this would help me to make enough milk for the baby."

Nettie usually left to go home after the baby was born and the breastfeeding was going smoothly. Mom told me, "Before Nettie had your daddy to take her home, she reminded me of some things to do to help the baby and to bring good luck. She told me to stay in the bed for nine days after the baby was born. The first three days I couldn't get up for nothin' except to use the pot. Nettie said that during those three days my womb was settlin' back in place, and I was to lay really still on the third day."

Mom continued, "After the third day of complete bed rest, I could get out of the 'living room' bed and sit in the 'big' rocker while I nursed the baby, but I shouldn't lift anything any heavier than my newborn."

Nettie's last words as she went out the door were a reminder to Mom about what she was supposed to do with the umbilical cord when it fell off the baby's belly. "Remember when the cord comes off naturally, you hold it between your thumb and fore finger over the top of the baby's head," she told Mom. "You take the cord around the baby's head three times and say, 'In the name of the father, the son, and the holy ghost,' then you burn the cord in the stove. This keeps evil and witches away."

In the days that followed, Mom used the "big" rocker as the center for nurturing and feeding the new baby. She rocked slowly back and forth, often crooning a lullaby as the baby filled its stomach with her rich and abundant supply of nourishment. Mom crooned some common lullabies to help the baby relax and fall asleep.

Rock a bye baby,
In the treetop.
When the wind blows,
The cradle will rock.
If the bough breaks,

The cradle will fall.
Down will come baby,
Cradle and all.

◆◆◆◆◆

Hush, little baby, don't say a word.
Daddy's gonna buy you a mockingbird

And if that mockingbird won't sing,
Daddy's gonna buy you a diamond ring

And if that diamond ring turns brass,
Daddy's gonna buy you a looking glass
And if that looking glass gets broke,
Daddy's gonna buy you a billy goat

And if that billy goat won't pull,
Daddy's gonna buy you a cart and bull

And if that cart and bull fall down,
You'll still be the sweetest little baby all around.

All along the Appalachian Mountains, women shared stories of the midwives in their communities. Midwives had their own families, but when a birth was about to happen, they fulfilled their duty. No matter the time of day or night, they packed their little black bag and often walked over the ridges to the home of the woman in labor. Midwives served a remarkable role in the whole tapestry of the community.

With the birth of a newborn baby and the mother's nine-day recovery, the "living room" bed had served one of its three main purposes. The next time a child used the living room bed was when common childhood diseases such as measles, mumps, or chicken pox occurred. Meanwhile, the "living room" bed was available for all other ailments that required warmth and loving care by family members.

Chapter 4

Gender Mattered

"Man is defined as a human being and a woman as a female–whenever she behaves as a human being she is said to imitate the male."

Simone De Beauvoir

When Nettie Conley stood at the foot of the "living room" bed and announced to Mom that her fourth baby was a "big healthy boy," all was right with the world. It really did matter whether the new baby was a boy or a girl. Mom was always disappointed in me because I was a girl, and she let me know how she felt for the remainder of her life. She said, "Well, I asked for a boy and you are what I got instead" so many times that I could hardly stand still and listen.

Most of my life I wanted to hit the world with both fists, but being a girl, I could not do that. Instead, I fought back in other ways. When I was a little girl, I tried to be a boy. I practiced until I thought I could walk like Freddie Heatwole, a classmate of mine. I dreamed of cutting my hair short like a boy. I was jealous of the simple little trousers and shirts my brothers wore. They dressed for school so fast my head spun. Their hair dried in no time and did not look bad if they did not comb it.

My brothers ran in packs with their friends and explored

the woods and fields far away from Mom's watchful eyes and screaming voice. They never had to touch a dirty dish or a dirty piece of clothing, mop the kitchen floor, sweep the porch, or tend to a baby's dirty diaper. They never canned a peach, tomato, or green bean, pickled a beet, or cut a head of cabbage for sauerkraut. At our house, my brothers never churned butter, fried an egg, peeled a potato, picked corn, or milked a cow. Mom did not allow them near the barn at milking time because she claimed they would upset the cows and they would not let their milk down. (When cows became nervous or scared, they refused to let their milk flow easily.) That was not good for the cows because they might go dry or get mastitis if they held on to their milk.

Fortunately, Mom meant no evil toward my sister or me. She loved both of us very much; however, from my perspective, she treated my brothers as if she loved them more. They always won her attention. Mom was a victim of the tradition of patriarchy that was pervasive in the Appalachian Mountains.

My mother was not the only one who treated her sons as privileged beings. A Kentucky friend of mine told me, "When Daddy came home from the hospital after Momma had a new baby, we asked him what it was. If it was a girl he said, 'Oh, it's just another pissy tail girl.'"

In my family when the midwife announced the arrival of a healthy baby girl, the word passed among the immediate and extended kin. Often the statement was, "Well, it's just another split-tale." Being a little girl with big ears, I certainly heard those comments and noted the disappointed facial expressions that went along with them.

"Split-tale" referred to the vagina. "God ran out of material when he made a girl," Mom explained to me when I was five years old. As she changed my brother's diaper, she pointed to his genitals and said, "See here. God sewed him up tight and this extra material hangs out. You don't have any extra material hanging out. God ran out of thread and didn't finish sewing you up."

I remember standing there looking at my brother and being quite aware that Mom was right–I was not sewn up nicely like my brother. I probably wondered to myself why God did not get more thread and material when he ran out. Why didn't God have enough to finish the job before he started? I certainly think I was too young at the time to think of myself as second-class or inferior to my brothers; however, that description and the special treatment given to boys finally sunk into my head.

Over the years, the messages about the lower rank of females in relation to males became more poignant and very mixed. Mom told me that menstruation was God's curse on Eve for tempting Adam to sin in the Garden of Eden. She told me that women were unclean during their period to the point that they could kill living plants simply by touching them. Every time one of her geraniums died, Mom blamed it on some woman who might have touched the plant when she stopped in to buy milk or homemade butter.

"I'll bet Mary [or Mamie or Ruby] was on her period when she touched my plant," Mom would complain. "I am gonna start tellin' women who come here not to touch my plants if they are 'thata way.'" She did, too. It was very embarrassing for the woman, whoever she was, and for me when I heard Mom say, "Mary, I hate to have to say this, but if you're at that time of the month, please don't touch my plants."

These women were our neighbors after we had moved out of Hopkins Gap to a less rural area, and so many of them never heard they were toxic during their periods. Their shocked reactions lead to a long story as to why they should not touch living plants.

Mom also told them that they should not be canning or preserving any foods while they were on their period. She stated her words of warning with the conviction of a true believer. The listeners were polite and then excused themselves. I am sure they never touched any of Mom's plants again whether they were on their period or not.

Mom could barely read because she had to quit school in the

fourth grade; however, she had taught herself to read over the years by reading romance magazines such as *True Confessions.* I often saw her sitting in the "big rocker" with the Bible in her lap. She frequently referred to "the truth" that was in the Bible as if she had read every word even though I did not think she read much of it. She never talked much about going to church when she was a child growing up in Hopkins Gap. The only Sunday she ever mentioned to me was one Sunday when she was about twelve years old. She stayed home from church and sold $270 worth of moonshine for Uncle Rob and Aunt Goldie. She grew scared when she realized how much money she had in the house. She grabbed the money, ran up the side of the mountain, and hid until she saw Uncle Rob and Aunt Goldie coming down the road from church. Since she spent her Sundays as a moonshine merchant, obviously she had heard the story of Adam and Eve as it had been passed down through her family.

Mom told me many times that women made men smell bad. She said, "Men don't stink unless they've been with a woman." As I grew older, I wondered how she knew what caused men to smell bad. According to her, "We wouldn't have sin in the world if Eve had behaved herself. Adam had a weak spot, and Eve knew how to tempt him. She offered him the apple, and he bit right into it without thinking. Men are weak when it comes to some things."

When Mom was not in her preaching mode, she told the Adam and Eve story in plain language and always blamed the woman for tempting the man into bad behavior. "A hard dick has no conscience, and it's up to the woman to control how a man acts. If she don't open the door, he can't walk in," she said. Mom blamed all adultery, fornication, premarital pregnancy, gonorrhea, syphilis, etc., on the female participant.

It was obvious that Mom thought women were stronger than men were and could control the moral fabric of the community if they stopped tempting men into sin. However, she treated my brothers and all men as if they were royalty. Was she protecting them because they were weak? Did she feel sorry for them?

A Woman's Hair is Her Glory?

Others also taught that men and women were different–and men were better. The traditional Mennonite church reinforced the idea that women were inferior to men based on a fundamentalist interpretation of the writings of St. Paul.

◆◆◆◆◆◆◆◆◆◆◆◆◆◆◆◆◆◆◆◆◆◆◆◆◆◆◆◆◆◆◆◆◆

St. Paul on Women . . .

St. Paul wrote that man is the head of the woman; man was not created for woman; but woman was created for man. Any woman who prays should keep her head covered, but men need not cover their heads. Women cannot speak in church. If they have a question, they should ask their husband at home. Women were saved through bearing children. These writings by St. Paul were fundamentally interpreted and taught to those who attended the traditional Mennonite church. These ideas led to behaviors such as: women wearing a covering on their heads, women sitting on one side of the church and men on the other, and women remaining silent in church. (5)

◆◆◆◆◆◆◆◆◆◆◆◆◆◆◆◆◆◆◆◆◆◆◆◆◆◆◆◆◆◆◆◆◆

Mom told me that it was in the Bible that a woman's long, shiny, and flowing hair tempted men to have sinful thoughts, so we had to cover our hair to protect them from sin. I thought that was the best argument for me to cut my hair short. Why forbid a female from cutting her hair when she had to stand in front of a mirror every morning and wind it up around her head and then put a covering over it?

Most men in my family forbade their wives and daughters from cutting their hair. My Grandpa John told Mom before he died, when she was nine years old, that she should never cut her hair, and she obeyed him until she was in her sixties. These orders never to cut her hair burdened her for many years because her hair grew until it reached below her knees.

This is a picture of Mom with the burdensome hairstyle that she wore most of her life. When she let her hair down, it reached below her knees.

On top of being long, Mom's hair was very thick. Washing it was a weekly chore. She had to use a washing tub in order to have enough water to wet it, soap it, and rinse it. Then she had to wear it down for most of the day so it could dry. After it dried, she began the long process of combing it out and of putting it up on top of her head as it is in the picture.

To achieve this bun, Mom started combing her hair on top of her head. With each stroke of the comb, she harvested a wad of hair that she carefully removed from the comb, wound around her finger, and then gathered into a loose ball. Throughout the tedious combing, Mom would occasionally get up and walk to the wood stove in the kitchen. I remember watching her take a ball of hair from the comb, lift the lid on the wood stove, and put it in the fire. The awful smell of Mom's hair burning in the stove would waft through the house and linger for a while. "You have to burn any hair that comes out when you comb because if a witch gets a hold of it, she can put a spell on you to give you headaches," she told me many times. "If a bird gets your hair and makes a nest out of it, your head will ache as long as the bird is using the nest."

After Mom combed the tangles out of the hair on top of her head, she worked her way down her thick and flowing mane. If she sat on a chair, the ends of her hair spilled all around her on the floor. Once she reached the middle level that flowed over her breasts, she held the combed hair in her left hand and pulled the ends up on her lap so she could comb them.

When the tangles were out of her hair, Mom used a roll made of cloth and stuffing that reached from ear to ear. She had bought several of these rolls at Woolworth. She placed the roll on the top of her head toward the front. Then she leaned over, put her forearms under her hair, and swept all of her hair back over the roll. She tucked the heavy hair behind the roll with hairpins. She took the long ends and twisted them with her hands, or braided them, and wound them across the back of her head at the nape of her neck. She kept all of that hair tucked in with long, sharp hairpins. I watched Mom many times as she put her hair up, and once said to her, "If you ever fall down, those hairpins will stick in your brain and kill you. You'd better be glad Dad doesn't hit you on the head when you boss him around." It took the best part of a whole day for Mom to wash her hair and put it up on top of her head. I often asked her why she did not have it cut off.

This is Mom as she proudly wears her short hair with a curly permanent. She appears happier with her heavy hair gone.

Sometime in her mid-sixties, Mom started having severe headaches. I asked her go to the doctor and ask if the weight of her hair could be the cause. Finally, after much pleading, she saw her doctor. He told her the headaches might be due to the weight of her hair. She came home all upset because her daddy had told her never to cut her hair.

I reminded Mom that her daddy had been dead over fifty years. I said, "Do you think if you could ask him, he would want you to suffer from headaches?" She thought about that for a while, and then she agreed to cut her hair and get a curly permanent.

When Mom came out of the beauty shop, she was ecstatic.

"I feel so light I think I could fly," she exclaimed. Her guilt for disobeying her daddy dissipated as the headaches disappeared and the time it took to care for her hair diminished to about twenty minutes.

Beastly Breast Contours and Ankles

Mom said it was also in the Bible that women had to wear long dresses to hide their breasts and ankles. Again, this was because men would look at them and have sinful thoughts. Of course, I thought that was the dumbest thing I had ever heard. When it was time for me to accept confirmation in the Mennonite church, Mom showed me several beautiful feed sacks that she was going to make into my "cape" dresses. "After you go up in front of the church and accept Jesus as your savior," she explained, "you will have to wear "cape" dresses to church with a prayer cap on your head."

I reflected on how hot and otherwise uncomfortable the Mennonite girls and women looked. Their dresses came so close to the tops of their shoes that you could barely see their feet. When the dress tail flopped up in the wind, I could see that they wore black stockings and black shoes.

Under the collars of their dresses, they had sewn a large piece of cloth of the same material that came out over their shoulders and down over their backs and chests. These were what Mom called "capes." For sure, the "capes" hid the contours of their breasts from any man who may have been tempted to look. I observed all of this and decided I was never going to go up to the front of the church and accept Jesus as my savior, and I refused when it was time for me to go.

Then there was the Sunday dinner table behavior–men received the call to the table to eat first while huge platters of fried chicken, heaping dishes of fluffy mashed potatoes, delicious green beans, gravy, fresh corn, and fried apples were still steaming. The table was a colorful work of art when they sat down to eat. The men had the privilege of being the first to dip into those beautiful dishes to fill their plates. The women stood around to make sure the men received all the food they wanted. When the men finished eating, they left the table and convened as a group in the living room or on the porch if the weather was warm.

After the men and children finished eating, the women sat down to eat the cold food left on the table. The beautiful platters of food were often empty and the ones that had food on them looked as if the chickens had been scratching in them. Many times, I saw Aunt Ethel and Mom chew on the chicken bones after the men and children had stripped most of the meat. That was all the meat they ate on those occasions. Therefore, a "man was a human being and a woman was a female" from the first appearance in the "living room" bed and throughout all aspects of life.

Chapter 5

Being One of Many

"He that raises a large family does, indeed, while he lives to observe them, stands a broader mark for sorrow; but then he stands a broader mark for pleasure too."

Benjamin Franklin

Appalachian Mountain families had many children. My own grandparents on my mother's side birthed eighteen children and raised twelve to adulthood, making them one of the largest of families. It was common for families along the Appalachian Mountain range to have fifteen, twelve, ten, nine, and eight children even in my generation. Very few families had less than five children.

The reasons for this were complex, but understandable. One of the major reasons was lack of access to and knowledge of birth control methods. Birth control pills were not available in the United States until 1963. Another reason included the belief that at least some of the children would die before their teenage years.

Aunt Goldie told me a story about my grandparents, John and Mary Morris, who had eighteen children. "Mom and Dad worried about having so many children," she said. "They tried 'pulling it out' [coitus interruptus] but Dad didn't wait long enough before he did it again." Some used folk remedies to try to stop pregnancy and a few used scary and dangerous ways to abort unwanted children.

Mountain families worked hard to survive in a sometimes harsh climate and geography. Men needed sons to help with the farming chores, such as butchering, as well as hunting for wild meat. Women needed daughters to help with the gathering, gardening, and preserving of food.

Pictured here are the youngest six of a family of ten children born to John William Bussey and his wife, Elizabeth Saul Bussey, of Franklin County, Virginia. The oldest four children have married and moved away from home to start their own families. (Picture courtesy of Pat Bussey.)

All children were expected to receive their nurturance and sustenance at the mother's breast. This was a convenient and inexpensive way to feed the babies because most mothers did not have wage-earning jobs outside the home. Taking care of a household, raising a garden, processing food, and tending to the needs of a large number of babies was about the only job a mother could handle. Therefore, in Mom's generation, many women saw no need to learn to drive a car. Later in Mom's life, she wished she had learned to drive because of the increased need for her to get to the drug store and the doctor. She had to depend on folks in the community who could drive.

Pictured here in 1949 are Thurman and Ella Harris with their ten children. The Harris family raised their children in a small log cabin in Patrick County, Virginia. (Picture courtesy of Peggy Harris).

While it took a lot of hard work to feed, clothe, and shelter a large number of children, there were certain times when having many brothers and sisters saved lives. Family members from Patrick County, Virginia, told a poignant story of how having a large number of brothers and sisters and a stay-at-home Mom saved the life of their little sister.

◆◆◆◆◆◆◆◆◆◆◆◆◆◆◆◆◆◆◆◆◆◆◆◆◆◆◆◆◆◆◆◆◆◆

Momma at the "Crosser"

One of the most beautiful features of the Appalachian Mountains is the plethora of small streams that drain water from the mountains and carry it through the valleys to the flatlands below. The rippling water of at least one of those streams soothed most mountain children to sleep each night and served as white noise that covered up the sounds of screech owls, barking dogs, and fighting cats that roamed in the dark.

Many children walked part of the way to school each day and often had to cross a stream to get to school or to the school bus stop. Some children were lucky enough to have a high footbridge to walk across the stream; others either jumped from rock to rock or took their shoes off and waded through the water during the warm seasons.

In all seasons of the year the water in mountain streams could suddenly rise, flow over its banks, and block schoolchildren away from home in the evening. In the spring and summer, the streams would rise because of melting snow or thunderstorms. In the fall, mountain streams would overflow their banks because of hurricanes that made landfall on the east coast and wound their way north into the Appalachian Mountains. Once in the mountains, such storms often became trapped and dumped large amounts of rain to be carried away by otherwise quiet little creeks.

This is precisely what happened on October 15, 1954. Hurricane Hazel came on shore as a Category Four storm in North Carolina. After damaging the beach, the hurricane moved rapidly up the east coast passing over the Appalachian Mountains, where it dumped record amounts of rain and packed hurricane force winds. Children who lived in the mountains had a perilous trip home from school that evening.

Schools didn't close in those days like they do now. We often went to school with snow falling, and stayed in school all day. The school bus trip home was often treacherous as the bus slid into ditches and hovered on the edges of deep hollows.

Peggy Harris, from Patrick County, Virginia, was the youngest of ten children. She is sitting on her mother's lap in the picture of the Harris family. Peggy related a story about how her life was saved on October 15, 1954 because she had many older brothers and sisters. The Harris family lived in an area of Patrick County called Shootin' Creek, which was named for a small stream.

High mountain springs fed the stream, and it afforded Peggy and her brothers and sisters a place to catch crawdads and play in the cool water in the summer time. Peggy played in Shootin' Creek with a pet duck, and she would go upstream and turn over rocks so that the water bugs beneath them could become a tasty morsel for the duck as it waited patiently below. "She always thanked me with a 'quack, quack' after she swallowed a bug," Peggy said.

Shootin' Creek separated the Harris family from the main road, and generally it ran low within its banks and caused no problems. The schoolchildren had to cross the water to get to the school bus stop. They walked across a low footbridge that they called a "crosser" in order to reach the path to their home. The "crosser" was a long log, hewed flat for safer footing, which had been placed across the creek. It had no handrails and rested no more than six inches above the water. Shootin' Creek often filled up and flooded the crosser even during a small summer thunder and lightning storm.

On October 15, 1954, all the children at Woolwine Elementary School watched as rain from Hurricane Hazel fall and the wind blew the trees outside their schoolhouse. The older Harris children worried as they thought about the water rising in Shootin' Creek. "I knew the creek was arisin', but I also knew that Momma would be waitin' for us on the other side. I felt pretty safe," Arlene, Peggy's sister, told me. "Mama was always there with coats when the weather changed–when it got cold during the day or when the creek was floodin', so we knew she would be there on that day."

At the end of the day, the school bus started winding its way over the high mountain roads. The wind had knocked down trees and tree limbs across the road. The older boys got off the school bus and moved the rubble so the bus could go around.

Finally, they reached the school bus stop. They stepped off the school bus and heard Shootin' Creek roaring in their ears as they rounded the first bend toward home. "The rain was pouring as if buckets were being emptied high in the sky. The wind bent and twisted the trees over our heads. Fall leaves were ripped from the limbs and whirled through the air," Peggy said.

As the children neared the creek, they saw the muddy water angrily tearing into the fragile banks on both sides of Shootin' Creek. They also saw that the crosser was covered. The older ones ran on across the log. "You could barely see where to put your feet," Arlene told me. She continued, "There was Mama on the other side with an arm full of coats and a broom. I wondered why she had brought a broom to the crosser. She was calling our names. I ran on across the creek."

Peggy added, "After the older ones went over the crosser, there were three of us left to get across. Suddenly we heard Mama calling us from the other end of the crosser. 'Hold hands and come on across before the water gets any deeper,' she screamed to us."

Peggy was only six years old and in the first grade. "I was really scared and started to scream and cry," she said. "Leonard and Donna tried to grab my hand, but I wouldn't let them lead me. I was scared they would let me fall into the muddy water."

She remembered looking at her mother's face. "I could tell she was scared, but only for a few seconds. She hardened her jaw and got into her "general" mode and started giving me orders. Momma yelled to me, 'Peggy, let Donna hold your hand, and I will meet you all half way.'"

She stopped screaming and did as she was told. Her brother, Leonard, stood behind her. "Momma turned around and grabbed an old cable that was tied to a limb on her side of the creek. She inched her way across the crosser toward us. While hanging onto the cable with one hand to steady herself, she held the broom handle in the other hand. When she got close enough, she raised the bristle end of the broom so that Donna could grab onto it," Peggy said.

"Donna had one hand holding the bristles on the broom, and one hand holding mine. Leonard grabbed my other hand, and we carefully placed one foot in front of the other until we reached Mama's open arms. She threw a coat over each of our heads, and we walked the long path home through the mud. I never forgot that day when Donna and Leonard kept me from drowning," Peggy recalled.

"I was so glad that Momma thought ahead enough to bring the broom. That's how she was all the time–always thinking about the right thing to do in any situation," Arlene added.

◆◆◆◆◆◆◆◆◆◆◆◆◆◆◆◆◆◆◆◆◆◆◆◆◆◆◆◆◆◆◆◆◆◆

Too Many Too Close

When the "living room" bed launched a new baby, the family greeted it with pride and happiness; however, it was commonly recognized and accepted that another child would soon come along to replace the new one. The last born often threw fits of jealousy when a new baby replaced him or her. Mom told me that I was miserable when my brother, Larry, was born. This lasted long enough for me to remember sitting on a kitchen chair in tears because I was upset about Larry's presence.

Anne Scott Pritchard breastfeeding her new baby while allowing her two-year-old son to return to the breast for nurturance.

I don't remember much about Brenda's birth, but my jealousy reappeared when my second brother, John, was born. The fact that he was a boy did not help the situation. I was five years old by this time. Mom asked me to help her take care of him. She put me in a rocking chair and tied a diaper around my waist and through the back of the chair so I wouldn't slide off. She laid John in my lap and asked me to hold him while she cooked supper. One time he slid off my lap and landed on his head on the hard kitchen floor. I don't recall her asking me to rock him after that occasion.

Breastfeeding continued for an average of eighteen months. Some children spoke of the closeness they felt with their mother when they were breastfeeding. Occasionally if the mother complied, the young child would partake of breast milk while the new baby nursed. I am sure this custom allowed for a better transition for the child from the center of attention as the youngest and last born to taking his or her place with the older children.

Being one of many children brought sorrow and joy. However, joy for both parents and children surpassed sorrow. On most occasions, many hands were needed to survive in isolated mountain communities. Parents hoped that each child would develop a specialty needed by the community and worked hard to teach their children. Their reward was the joy of hearing their neighbors talk about their sons and daughters as great workers and providers for their families.

Chapter 6

Birth Order

"Making the decision to have a child–it's momentous. It is to decide forever to have your heart go walking outside your body."

Elizabeth Stone

Being one of many children born in the "living room" bed allowed the consequences of a child's place in the birth order to become clearer in his or her personality. All along the Appalachian Mountains from Grayson County to Rockingham County, Virginia, folks described similar experiences of oldest, middle, and youngest children.

Being the Oldest Child

Being the oldest child had advantages and disadvantages. Shirley, the oldest daughter of ten children growing up in Patrick County, Virginia, related how she really did not have a childhood. "Momma just kept on having babies after me. She needed me to help her. I remember ironing clothes when I was so young I had to stand on a chair to reach the ironing table. I heated the irons on the stove. When one got cold, I jumped down off the chair and put it back on the stove and got the hot one. I kept on ironing until it was done."

Pat from Franklin County, Virginia, talked about her oldest sister, whom she called, "a mother to all of us. Momma was so busy trying to keep all of fed and warm, that she had to depend on Anna for help."

For me, the eldest of five, the advantage was that I was more likely to get new clothes than I was to get hand-me-downs. "I wanted everything new for you," Mom said, "so I bought you a little blue snow suit, a bunch of dresses, and some little white leather shoes. I sewed your gowns, diapers, and bellybands. I was so proud of you. We took you to a studio in Harrisonburg to have your first picture made when you were just eleven weeks old."

My sister, Brenda, had to wear my hand-me-downs, and she still complains about never having a new store-bought dress or a dress that was handmade just for her when she was a child. Many of the clothes we wore were made out of feed sacks. The girls in the family had to share clothes after they started school. This was one of the main reasons that my sister and I fought each other. When we were in high school, we had two skirts, a few blouses, and one sweater called a "Sloppy Joe." It was the only piece of in-style clothing that we had. We had begged Mom to buy us a "Sloppy Joe" so we would be like the other girls in school, and we had promised we would share it.

We took turns wearing it, but we didn't always agree on who had worn it last. The result was blood-curdling fights in the morning before school. These fights occurred while Mom was at the barn milking her cows. Since she wasn't in the house, we hit, scratched, and pulled hair. I usually won those fights because I was naturally stronger.

Mom knew we were fighting because our collie dog, Toby, ran around the outside of the house barking his head off when we did. Worse yet, we knew that she knew we were fighting, but we also knew she couldn't leave her cows halfway milked and come to the house. We made sure our fights ended just before she opened the kitchen door. One morning, however, Brenda had obviously been practicing her fighting skills or eating her Wheaties. She turned on me. When she finished with me, I handed over the piece of clothing she wanted to wear that day. That incident ended our fighting, at least over clothes.

The oldest child received less attention from its parents. This was a big disadvantage. After my younger brothers and sister were born, I tried every way I could to get Mom's positive attention. For example, when I went out in the yard to play under the black cherry tree, I kept my eyes on the kitchen door for Mom to step out and check on me. If she had to yell at Larry and Brenda when she came out, I would say, "Look at me, Mom. Look at how good I am being today." She was so busy yelling at them that she never paid any attention to me.

Because I was the first born, family circumstances caused me to have too much responsibility at a very young age. My daddy was drafted into the Army in August of 1944 as part of the replacement for the soldiers killed at the Normandy Beach invasion in June of that year. He was drafted in spite of the fact that he had three small children. My sister, Brenda, was only six weeks old when he left. I was three, and my brother, Larry, was twenty-two months old.

We lived far out in the country away from a doctor. There were no such things as preschool or day care, so Mom was responsible for us twenty-four hours a day, seven days a week. Luckily, she was renting a house from a wonderful farmer and his wife, Pop and Minnie May. Pop May gave her a cow so she would have milk for us to drink; however, that meant she had to milk the cow twice a day.

While my sister was a small baby, Mom took all of us to the barn with her when she went to milk the cow. Larry was learning to walk, so the trip to the barn was very slow. Mom carried two small baby bottles with nipples with her. She laid the baby across her lap. Larry and I stood beside her while she milked. The first thing she did was fill the baby bottles with warm milk straight from the cow's teat. We stood there and sucked the bottles. Mom filled them up as fast as we emptied them.

When the baby grew too big to lie across her lap, she put all three of us into the baby bed and told me to watch them while she went to the barn to milk. I was about three-and-a-half years old. I vaguely remember feeling very responsible for Larry and Brenda's safety. When Mom came in from the barn, she bragged on what a good babysitter I was. She told Aunt Goldie, "Peggy watches the young ones for me. Nobody has moved an inch when I get in from the barn."

My daddy wanted a boy for his first-born, and my mother wanted to give him a son as the oldest child. Mom actually had a physical description in mind for her first-born son. In her mind, he would have a full head of black hair and brown eyes. She was going to name him William. Unfortunately, I was born with thin blond hair and very blue eyes and I was female. My brother, Larry, came eighteen months after me. He was exactly what Mom wanted her first-born to be. He had a full head of black hair, and eventually his eyes turned a dark brown. Someone in the family had already used her desired name, so she called him Larry. Mom fussed over him; he was perfect. "I want to be a boy with black hair and brown eyes," I told her.

"Well, that's what I wanted and I got you instead," she replied. I think some of those attitudes about wanting a boy as the first-born still live on today.

To the end of her days on this earth, I always tried to please Mom. I listened carefully to what she wanted or needed. If she said, "I would like to have a lot of strawberries this coming spring," I located a good source for berries. Many times, I picked strawberries in Salem and drove them to Harrisonburg so that Mom would have what she wanted. Often, she told me, "These are really nice berries, but Larry just brought me five gallon yesterday." I guess Larry was doing the same thing–trying to get attention from Mom since she had three more children after he was born.

Being the Middle Child

Being the middle child is the most unenviable position into which a person can be born. No one suffered more than my sister, Brenda, who was born in the exact middle of five children. She didn't get off to a good start, and remained prone to accidents and childhood illnesses. The only benefit for Brenda was that she recovered from her maladies in the "living room" bed.

Brenda was just six weeks old when Dad was drafted into the army. By that time, she had already been injured, the victim of a large rat that crawled into the house, jumped up into her baby bed, and bit several holes in her tiny hand. Dad chased the rat out of the house, but it returned for more blood. Finally, he trapped it in the kitchen under Mom's sauerkraut jar and killed it with a stick.

While Dad was in the army, Brenda had two serious scrapes with death. Mom, Larry, and I all slept in the "living room" bed while Dad was away. Brenda slept in a baby bed beside the living room bed. She was a curious child and started crawling and sliding on her rear end at about nine months old. One day, Brenda crept behind the stove where Mom kept a tin can of kerosene for lighting the morning fire. She found the can, turned it up to her lips, and took a swig of kerosene. She strangled, of course, and sucked some of the kerosene into her lungs.

Brenda got pneumonia from her little excursion behind the kitchen stove. Mom refused to let the doctor admit her to the hospital, so my first memory of Brenda was of her being sick. Mom walked the living room floor with her night after night as she lay across her shoulder grunting for every breath. When she wasn't walking the floor, Mom held Brenda on her lap in the "big rocker" that sat beside the "living room" bed and hummed lullabies to her.

During the first days of Brenda's sickness, Aunt Goldie drove to Hopkins Gap and picked up some skunk grease from Grandma Molly. Mom rubbed it on a heated red-flannel rag, and put it on Brenda's chest. She lit an old lamp she had after filling it with cresoline.

◆ ◆

Vapo-Cresoline Lamp . . .

This lamp belonged to Mom. She used it to burn cresoline (a liquid coal tar substance) when someone in the family had whooping cough or pneumonia. Cresoline was available at drug stores. Mom poured the liquid in the pan at the top of the lamp. She lit the small lamp at the bottom and sat the lamp next to the "living room" bed where the sick person slept. The heat from the small lamp released fumes from the coal tar.

The Vapo-Cresoline lamp was manufactured in 1879 after a man ran out of options for treating his daughter, who had pneumonia. He placed liquid coal tar in a tin cup, and placed it over a candle. He claimed the vapors from the coal tar saved his daughter's life; thus he discovered a commercial product—the Vapo-Cresoline lamp. The lamp was sold until the 1930s in the U.S. At that time, the U.S. Food and Drug Administration ended the production and sale of the lamp on the claim that it healing properties were false. (6)

◆ ◆

The lamp gave off fumes that were supposed to open up Brenda's chest. The smell was horrible. I was scared. Mom was crying because she feared Brenda was going to choke to death from the pneumonia. I remember she stopped crying and started to sing a lullaby. The combination of warm skunk grease and cresoline fumes, the baby grunting for her breath, the creaking of the "big rocker," and Mom's crying and singing, kept me awake.

◆ ◆

Skunk Grease . . .

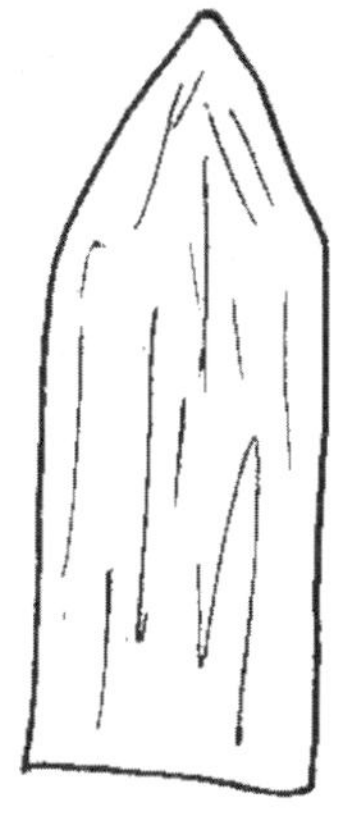

Skunk grease was made from the fat of a skunk. Mountain men hunted skunks at night and sold their skins for a little extra income. When they arrived home with their kill, they skinned the skunks and stretched their hides, inside out, over a board that was designed to keep the skin stretched. The pointed part of the board was where the skunk's head had been, and the wider end of the board stretched the belly and hind legs of the skunk skin. The tail was left on the skin. The skunk boards were hung on the outside of an outbuilding until they dried and were ready to sell.

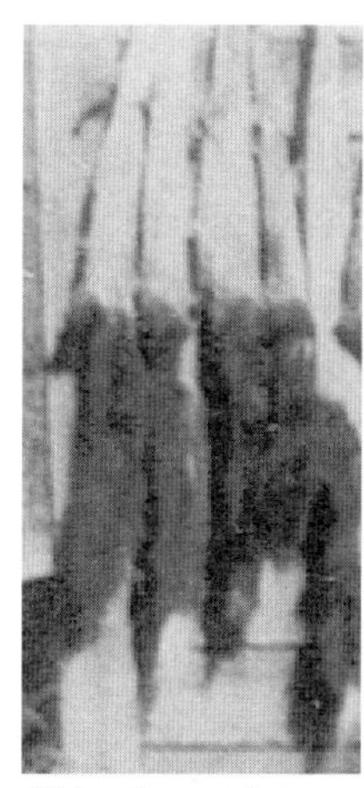

This picture shows some of Uncle Shirley's skunk skins as they are drying for the market.

As soon as the skins were stretched, the woman of the house scraped the lumps of fat off the inside of the skin. She placed the fat in an old iron skillet and heated it until the lumps gave off a liquid fat. She squeezed the lumps until she got all the liquid fat that she could. The liquid fat was set aside and allowed to cool until it turned into the consistency of a salve. This skunk grease was rubbed on a warm red-flannel cloth and placed on the chest as a decongestant.

◆ ◆

Brenda recovered from pneumonia and went on to explore her surroundings as she learned to walk. Her next adventure was the discovery of a light bulb. In those days, there were no warnings about keeping dangerous things away from children. Houses had few closets or cabinets and even fewer storage areas out of the reach of curious youngsters.

Somehow, Brenda carried a light bulb up Aunt Goldie's stair steps, where she dropped it. The bulb shattered into tiny slivers of glass. She stepped in it and cut her feet. Then she decided to taste it and put some in her mouth. Brenda never made a sound as blood ran down her lower lip. Mom screamed when she found her. The screaming scared Brenda, so she started bawling. It was a bloody mess, and Aunt Goldie had to drop whatever she was doing and drive Brenda all the way to Broadway to see Dr. Watson. He cleaned the glass off her tongue and recommended Merthiolate for the cuts on her feet. (Merthiolate is an antiseptic used by mothers for many years. It was banned from use because of its mercury content.)

One day, Mom went to the wood yard to chop wood for the stoves. She told me to watch Brenda, who was nearly two years old by now and walking quite well. She was still into everything. Mom had left a pot of ham boiling on the kitchen stove. Brenda went into the kitchen, dragged a chair over to the stove, and climbed up to the boiling pot. She grabbed the edge of the pot and burned her fingers. She didn't know to let go of the boiling pot, so she pulled it off the stove as she fell from the chair. I heard her scream and ran to the kitchen. She was floating on her belly in the scalding broth on the kitchen floor. I was only five, and I wasn't able to get to her to pull her away. I ran to the front door to get Mom. I couldn't reach the latch, so I started screaming and pounding on the door. Mom heard me and ran in the house. She found Brenda floating in the hot broth. She grabbed her up and ran across the hill to Aunt Goldie's house–about a half-mile. Aunt Goldie took her to the doctor, another twenty-five miles away. The trip was long and over a dirt road. Brenda had third-degree burns on her belly; she carries the scar to this day.

My dad was still fighting in World War II when Brenda had pneumonia, ate the light bulb, and scalded her belly. When it was time for his return, Mom moved us children from the "living room" bed into a bedroom just off the living room. The bedroom was separated from the living room by a flimsy cloth curtain so that heat from the living room stove could keep us warm. Mom continued to sleep in the "living room" bed. When Dad arrived home from the war one night, he was too exhausted to take off his uniform so he lay down on top of the covers on the "living room" bed. I woke up the next morning to find him asleep with his arm around Mom.

Brenda climbed out of bed and came to the door between the bedroom and the living room. She had no idea who Dad was because she was only six weeks old when he had left for the army. Brenda wrapped her arms around the cloth curtain and started to suck her thumb as she stared at the man lying across the "living room" bed. When Dad awoke, he saw her. He stared at her for a few seconds. "Who is that? That's the ugliest kid I ever saw," he said to Mom.

"Well, Norman, that's Brenda. She looks exactly like you," Mom replied. Brenda did look like Dad, and she still does to this day; however, that moment at the bedroom door shaped his relationship with Brenda. Because he had not bonded with her as a baby, he always treated her differently from the rest of us children.

Not long after Dad came home, we all became sick with the whooping cough. Two of us quickly recovered, but Brenda got a very bad case of it. She would go into coughing spasms and lose her breath. Mom had to reach into her throat with her finger to pull the phlegm out so that she could get her breath. One day Brenda was especially sick and Mom couldn't get the phlegm out with her finger. She screamed at Dad, "Do something. She is choking to death!" Dad grabbed Brenda and ran outside into the cold air.

In his panic, he started running up the road toward Aunt Goldie's house. The cold air forced little Brenda to grab for her breath. The phlegm shot out of her mouth and ran down the back of Dad's shirt. She had survived another spasm of coughing.

Larry and I were very grossed out at the sight of the whooping cough phlegm that came out of Brenda's throat. We labeled her dirty, and we refused to eat after her or drink out of a cup or glass that we saw her use–even though it might have been washed a thousand times.

Typical of the middle child, Brenda was plagued by a severe need for attention from our parents. This meant Larry and I did not like to play with her, because we didn't trust that she could keep secrets from Mom and Dad. One day, when I was about seven years old, we had a visit from the Turner children. They rode the school bus with us, and invited themselves over to play one day after school was out.

We told Mom we were going down over the hill in Pop May's pasture. She said, "Why don't you take Brenda with you?" My sister jumped up and down with the thought of getting to play with us. We growled but finally said she could come.

We crossed the fence, and as we walked down the hill, Roscoe Turner kept looking back toward our house. When he thought he was far enough down the hill so we couldn't be seen, he reached into his overalls pocket and pulled out a pack of cigarettes and matches to light them. I knew that I wanted to smoke, and I knew Larry wanted to smoke, too. We had been sneaking around and smoking Dad's old *Lucky Strike* butts, and we had discussed how good a whole new cigarette might taste. Here we were with the perfect opportunity to try a whole new cigarette, but we had Brenda with us.

I glanced at Larry and we both knew we were going to get a whipping if Mom found out we were smoking. Brenda watched us as we pondered the situation. "Bren, will you tell Mom on us if we smoke?" I said to her.

"No, I won't tell," she quickly replied. My mind flashed back over other times when she had promised not to tell and then went straight home and told on us. The whole new cigarette that Roscoe had handed me was burning my sweating palm. I wanted it bad, but I didn't want a whipping.

Then I had a brilliant idea. I looked at Brenda and said, "We'll let you have a puff if you promise not to tell, so if you do tell, you will get a whipping too. I'll tell Mom you smoked along with us."

"Yeah, I'd like a puff," she said, "and I won't tell."

Roscoe, Larry and I each lit up a whole new cigarette. I took a few drags and then handed the cigarette to Brenda. This moment was a testament to the great power of nicotine because we had to forget about the whooping cough phlegm that had shot from her mouth a long time ago. Brenda took a big puff off the cigarette and accidentally inhaled it. She started coughing and ran straight up the hill to the house. Unbeknownst to us, she told Mom that we were down the hill smoking and had forced her to take a puff so she wouldn't tell on us.

Meanwhile, we continued to enjoy our cigarettes while Mom pulled a switch off the lilac bush. She crossed the fence and screamed from the crest of the hill, "You all come up here. I'm gonna switch the piss out of you."

We all slowly walked up the hill. Roscoe put the cigarettes back in his pocket. "I hope she don't beat my ass," he said.

"She probably will," I told him.

When we got close enough for her to grab us, she reached into Roscoe's pocket and confiscated his remaining cigarettes. "You get your ass on home now and don't you ever come back," she yelled at him. "I am gonna tell your daddy on you." She grabbed my arm and switched my legs until I thought I was going to wet my pants.

"I'll teach you to smoke cigarettes. When I get done with you, you will never want another one," she shouted. She grabbed Larry once she had finished pummeling me. She lashed his legs with the switch.

When we got our breath back, we simultaneously yelled, "Brenda was smokin' too."

"Don't try to drag her into your meanness," she snorted.

We were curious about her answer. Did Brenda tell on us or not? Then we asked, "Did Brenda tell you we was smokin'?"

"No, she didn't tell. I came out on the porch to check on you all and saw a cloud of smoke streamin' into the air. I didn't know what was going on until I peeked over the hill," Mom said.

Later, we learned that Brenda had told on us and that Mom had fibbed about seeing a puff of smoke. By the time we found out the truth, we had forgotten the pain of the lilac switch on our legs. I figured that Mom lied about Brenda tattling on us to protect her from our wrath. Even though we didn't know for sure that Brenda blabbed her mouth to Mom, we never let her go with us again because we knew that she felt so guilty when she did something bad that she would tell Mom immediately.

The next tragic event in Brenda's young life was a broken leg. We were playing in Aunt Goldie's peach orchard when she spotted a beautiful peach on the highest limb of a peach tree. Against my sisterly advice, she started to climb the tree. Halfway up to the peach, Brenda realized she couldn't go any further. She turned around to come down out of the tree and got scared. She started crying. I said, "Here, let me lean over and you can jump on my back."

Brenda jumped onto my back, rolled to the ground, and started screaming. Mom rushed to the orchard to see what had happened. Brenda's right leg was twisted in a scary way. She had split a bone in her lower leg. Aunt Goldie cranked up her pickup truck and off they went to Broadway to see Dr. Watson once more.

While Brenda's leg was in a cast, Mom let her sleep in the "living room" bed to protect her. However, this did not help her stay safe and by the end of the first week, she was sliding around the house on her butt. Somehow, she convinced me to pull her around in a little red wagon.

We were all playing on the cement-slab front porch one day when my cousin, George, pulled up in front of the house. He was just learning to drive, so he was excited about driving across the hill from Aunt Goldie's house to our house to borrow something from Mom. He jumped out of the car and rushed into the house. Meanwhile, I pulled Brenda in front of the car, became distracted by something else, and forgot she was sitting in harm's way.

George came rushing out of the house and jumped in the car without looking. He started the motor, and I realized Brenda was in front of him. I started screaming, "Stop, stop. Brenda's in the way!" It was too late. George started forward and ran into the red wagon with Brenda in it. The wagon tipped over and made a loud noise. George realized he had hit something and stopped. Brenda started screaming. She was pinned under the wagon, but escaped with a crushed cast on her leg and a badly skinned big toe. George went home to get Aunt Goldie, and Brenda went back to Broadway to see Dr. Watson. Mom told me, "Dr. Watson just shook his head and said her broken leg had healed enough that he didn't have to change the cast." I think that if all that stuff happened to a child today, the doctor would report somebody for child abuse. However, no one was abusing Brenda but Brenda.

When Brenda was in grade school and high school, she was an insecure student and wanted to get good grades. She carried all of her schoolbooks with her when Dad took us for a ride on Sundays, or when we went to Hopkins Gap to visit Grandma Molly. Brenda tried to do her homework in the back seat of the car. Larry and I made fun of her and called her "Miss Library." She ignored us and kept trying to do her work. I know now that she probably wanted Mom and Dad to think highly of her for being dedicated to her schoolwork.

The merciless teasing of Brenda continued into her high school years and after she started dating the boy she eventually married. I told her that if her boyfriend blew his nose, she needed to get out of the car or she would get pregnant. "Is that true?" she said.

"Yes it is true," I assured her.

"Who told you that?"

"Mom told me that a long time ago." That answer convinced her to believe me.

When we were older, she told me that when her boyfriend reached in his pocket for his handkerchief to blow his nose, she was too embarrassed to get out of the car; however, she did worry about getting pregnant. She almost stopped dating him. Finally, she got up enough nerve to ask Mom if what I had told her was true. To this day, Brenda occasionally reminds me of how uncomfortable I made her feel when she was dating.

Being the Youngest Child

In very large families, frequently the older children married and left home while the mother was still birthing babies. This was the case with Pat, who grew up in Franklin County, Virginia, and Peggy, who grew up in Patrick County, Virginia.

Pat told me that her life was very different from mine because she was the youngest child of ten. Her mother was in her late forties when she was born. "They called me a 'change-of-life' baby," she said. "The doctor begged Momma to have an abortion. He told her I would be either very intelligent or very retarded and the chances were great that I would be retarded."

Her mother refused the doctor's advice, saying, "I will take what God gives me," according to Pat.

"When the labor pains started for me, the old doctor, who lived about three miles away, rode his horse to our home for my birth. I was born in the 'living room' bed. Momma was really sick after I was born. She hemorrhaged and the doctor barely saved her life. Momma was too weak for several weeks to do anything but nurse me," Pat reported.

Her oldest sister, Anna, took over the care of her sister as well as the housework. "Six months later Momma was diagnosed with stomach cancer," Pat said. "She went to Roanoke, Virginia, to the hospital. Roanoke was about thirty miles away, but at that time, it might as well have been on the other side of the world. Daddy didn't have a car so we could visit Momma. She was gone from our home for a full year."

Anna taught Pat how to drink from a bottle, and then how to walk and talk. "When Momma came home, I thought Anna was my mother," Pat said. However, life eventually returned to the way it was before her mother's illness. The family worked the farm, milked the cows, and planted a huge vegetable garden so they could can the garden produce.

"My older brothers and sisters started to leave home to find jobs, get married, and start their own families. I was devastated," Pat recalled. "I cried as each one left home. I was nervous and bit my fingernails down into the flesh."

The older siblings returned every Sunday for dinner. Pat's parents lived in a home with a huge kitchen with a wood cooking stove. The dinner table, which had a large bench behind it for the children, held fifteen people at a time. "The food was fresh from the garden in the summer time and from the cellar in the winter," Pat said. "Momma always cooked beef, pork, and chicken along with at least eight or ten different vegetables. She baked a huge cake and at least twelve fruit pies. Momma cooked most of the food before she went to church. We walked a mile to church. We filled that dinner table up three times with family. I was very happy when the table was full. My sister Anna and later I was responsible for keeping the dishes clean for the next group to eat."

By this time, Pat had youngsters close to her age to play with as her older brothers and sisters had children of their own. "We had a good time playing and being together. My nieces and nephews also went to the same school as I did. They teased me by threatening to call me 'Aunt Pat' at school. I swore I would hurt them if they called me 'Aunt Pat,' because it made me feel really old," Pat said.

"At the end of the day on Sundays, everybody left to go to their own homes. I dreaded the end of the day. Sunday became a day of leaving and sadness. Momma loved to have all her children around her. She cried after everybody was gone, and I crawled up in her lap as she sat on the 'big rocker' by the 'living room' bed. I cried myself to sleep."

One of Pat's brothers died in a car wreck on his twenty-first birthday. "Momma never recovered from his death. I remember going to the cemetery with her. She cried and talked to my brother as if he were alive," she said.

Four of Pat's brothers went off to fight in World War II. Pat's mother, "walked the floor and cried if she didn't get a letter from them. I walked along with her and cried too. I missed them coming home on Sunday. We were all so close," she said.

The four men returned safely. They found work and bought cars. "Life got easier for all of us. I began to benefit more from being the youngest child. My brothers all started dating and hired me to polish their shoes. I got twenty-five cents a pair. They took me with them on their dates. We went to get ice cream or to a movie," she remembered.

Her father became ill with bone cancer when he was seventy-five years old. "He lay down in the 'living room' bed and Momma cared for him," Pat said. Her older siblings wondered what would become of their mother if their father did not recover. "She always said, 'Don't worry about me. I am going with him,'" Pat recalled.

"One day Daddy got really sick and was taken from the 'living room' bed to the hospital. He had had a stroke. Daddy didn't make it and, sure enough when Daddy died, Momma died the next day. She was talking on the phone when the main artery in her heart exploded. Daddy was buried on Tuesday and Momma was buried on Wednesday," Pat said.

"Being the youngest child allowed me to have a lot of mommas and daddies. I felt very special. Now, I am able to return to the love and care that I received from my older brothers and sisters. I spend a lot of my retirement time taking care of them as they need me," Pat said.

Peggy grew up in Patrick County, Virginia as the youngest of ten children. "When my older sisters, Shirley and Arlene, got married, I cried for days," said Peggy. "They were the only ones who ever gave me any attention. Momma was so busy taking care of all of us that she never had time to sit down and hold me on her lap. My older brother, Ronnie, told me recently that he never knew I existed. He said, 'All I remember about you is a little girl sitting in the corner reading a book and never saying a word to anybody. It's nice to get to know you now that we are getting older.'"

Just like Pat, Peggy said she looked forward to Sunday dinner when her older brothers and sisters came home to eat, but she also dreaded the evening when they left again. "It was really lonely after they left especially in the summer time when I didn't have school to look forward to the next day," she said. "Finally, in the evening, it was just me and Momma holding down the fort."

Mountain parents probably wondered why their children were sometimes very different from one another. However, these differences did not matter. They loved each and every child and cared for them when they were sick and remembered those who died, regardless of their ages. Pat of Franklin County, Virginia, and Peggy of Patrick County each lost a brother to car accidents. Both talked of the life-long grieving of their mothers.

Chapter 7

Many Aunts, Uncles, and Cousins

"The hardest arithmetic to master is that which enables us to count our blessings."

Eric Hoffer

Children in my generation arrived in the "living room" bed having inherited large numbers of aunts and uncles. This was a common pattern all along the Appalachian Mountains. Peggy of Patrick County, Virginia, had a total of fifteen aunts and uncles. When I asked her how many first cousins she had, she said, "I never counted them, but I am sure I had a very lot." Pat of Franklin County, Virginia, had around eighteen aunts and uncles. She never met most of them because she was a menopause baby. Her aunts and uncles died before she was born. She did not count her first cousins either.

In my case, I had nine aunts and uncles from my Dad's side of the family, and eleven from my Mom's side. That made a total of twenty aunts and uncles for me and my brothers and sister.

Each one of my aunts and uncles influenced my life, but a few of the more important ones were on my Mom's side of the family. Mom's sisters, Aunt Goldie and Aunt Dorothy, and her brother, Uncle Shirley, taught me some of the lessons of life. Most of the other aunts and uncles were not as close or had moved away from Hopkins Gap when I was very young.

Aunt Goldie

Aunt Goldie was closer to me than any other aunt or uncle because she raised my mother after she was orphaned at age nine. I loved her like the grandmother I never knew and would have died for her. On one occasion during a major snowstorm, I learned how important Aunt Goldie really was to me.

It used to snow a lot in the wintertime when I was a kid growing up in the mountains. It was not unusual for a storm to drop eighteen to twenty-five inches of snow followed by two days of strong winds. The temperature was very cold, so the snow was fluffy and light. Folks often got their cars stuck in the snow and had to walk to find shelter. Once, Aunt Goldie was stuck about a mile below our house. It was snowing hard and the wind was howling. She was blinded by the snow, but she finally found her way to our front door. When she came in the house, her face was blue and red from the snow. She had ice in her hair and her clothes were frozen. Tears streamed down her cheeks. She sobbed as she rubbed her stiff, blue hands together. "I thought I was gonna freeze," she cried. "I couldn't see where I was going on the road, so I got up on the bank and followed the fencerow. If I had to go any further, I would have died out there."

Mom had Aunt Goldie to take off her wet clothes. She gave her a clean flannel nightgown and put her into the warm "living room" bed. Aunt Goldie calmed down and fell asleep. She stayed at our house until the roads were cleared the next day.

I will never forget how scared she looked as she stood shivering beside our living room stove. I had nightmares about Aunt Goldie freezing to death for several weeks. In one of my nightmares, Aunt Goldie was standing at the foot of her staircase. She was crying because she didn't have any money. I gave her nine pennies and told her that was all I had to give her.

Aunt Goldie was very special to me because she always made me feel good about myself. She told me I was a good worker and that I had pretty handwriting when she had me write her letters. Aunt Goldie had dropped out of school in the third grade. She couldn't read or write.

Waking Up to Aunt Dorothy

The day started early in the mountains. Most children had chores to do before school, such as milking the cow, feeding the chickens, and slopping the hogs. Sometimes adult activities disrupted our sleep during the night. In particular, late night fights resulted in the arrival of a mother and her children who ran to escape the beatings of a drunken husband. This did not happen in all families, and it didn't happen every night. But when it did happen, it was usually very memorable.

Before we moved from our four-room house with the cement-slab front porch, Mom, Dad, and all of us children slept in the same room. Mom had moved the "living room" bed out of the living room because Dad "wallowed all over it" every chance he got. She did not like the covers of the "living room" bed to be all messed up. Mom moved the bed where she and Dad slept into the bedroom by the front window. Brenda, Larry, and I slept in a double bed near the wall on the opposite side of the room. The baby, John, slept in a crib next to Mom and Dad's bed.

We didn't have a doorbell, so when anyone needed to contact us in the middle of the night, they pecked on the window over Mom and Dad's bed. On many occasions, the pecking was Aunt Dorothy.

"Myrtle, Myrtle," Aunt Dorothy would yell as she sobbed. "Please let us in. Olin is drunk, and he beat me up. I have all the kids with me." It was usually very cold outside and sometimes it was raining. It seemed to me when I was a child that Olin Kephart liked to drink more on cold or rainy nights. I recently learned from Aunt Dorothy's third child, Mildred, that Olin Kephart drank all the time–even in warm weather. On warm nights, Aunt Dorothy took the children outside into a hayfield and slept there with them until he sobered up.

Dad would cuss a little when he heard Aunt Dorothy. "Damn it, Myrt. I'm getting' tired of this shit all the time," he'd say.

Mom would groan as she sat up in bed. "What the hell am I supposed to do? I can't let her and the kids freeze," she'd reply. Then she would shuffle out of the bedroom and unlatch the front door.

Aunt Dorothy always apologized to Mom, "I'm sorry Myrtle. I don't know why he drinks so much."

Mom would get out extra comforters. Then she would ask the two oldest children, "Do you all have to use the pot?"

"No," they would answer.

Mom would say, "Well you use it anyway." After they used the pot, she would put them on the couch, with the oldest girl with her head on one end and the oldest boy's head on the other end. She covered them up with a comforter. She placed the next three children in our bed. Two heads at the bottom of the bed and one head at the top of the bed with us. That made five children in one bed.

The children were always cold when they got in bed with us. Mom handed Aunt Dorothy two comforters and told her to make a bed on the dining room floor. She slept there with her baby. In a matter of ten minutes, the house would be quiet once again. Many times all this activity happened and I never heard a bit of it. I would wake up the next morning with a putrid smell invading my nose. When that happened, I knew that Aunt Dorothy and her children had arrived during the night. The kids had a distinct odor–grease and cigarette smoke–and it wafted from under the covers.

Mom knew she had to make more breakfast, so she woke up earlier to milk the cow and cook. She made sausage gravy and fried eggs. Aunt Dorothy put the kids up to the table to eat. Generally, all but one of them ate like they were starving. After her kids ate what they wanted, Aunt Dorothy took a heel of bread from the bread plate and sopped up little bits of gravy from each of her children's plates. That was all I ever saw her eat.

Mildred did not eat. She said, "I ain't hungry," and hung her head. She was next in age to the two oldest children. I remember studying her face and wondering if she was ashamed that she smelled bad and had to get up and leave home in the middle of the night.

Aunt Dorothy finally lost her children to Social Services. All six of them were taken away one day. The two oldest were taken to Lynchburg Training School in Lynchburg and immediately sterilized so they couldn't have children. The four youngest–two boys and two girls–were placed in foster care.

◆◆◆◆◆◆◆◆◆◆◆◆◆◆◆◆◆◆◆◆◆◆◆◆◆◆◆◆◆◆◆◆◆◆

Eugenics Movement Touches Hopkins Gap . . .

Eugenics is the study and practice of selective breeding applied to humans, with the aim of improving the species. The idea of eugenics had been put forward in 1883. The trend first became popular in Europe and then found followers in the United States.

In 1924, the Commonwealth of Virginia adopted a statute authorizing the compulsory sterilization of the mentally retarded for the purpose of eugenics. The statute became popular and was used throughout the United States.

The plan of the compulsory sterilization statute was to stop the breeding of "unfit" people so that the state's burden of unfit individuals, who would need institutionalization for life, would eventually diminish. It was believed that the "poor" had genes for feeblemindedness, which led them to misery, vice, and crime; thus, the obvious solution to American social problems was to sterilize them.

The Virginia location for compulsory sterilization was in Lynchburg. It was called at various times the Virginia State Epileptic Colony and Lynchburg State Colony for Epileptics and Feeble-Minded, and was the largest institution of its kind in the United States. It opened in 1910 and became a dumping ground for Virginia's poorest residents, teens from broken homes, and others whom state officials considered socially inadequate. From the 1920s until 1972, the Lynchburg hospital sterilized some 4000 patients. Most had no idea that they were being sterilized. Most had not given their consent for the surgical procedures that the hospital put them through.

During the mid-1950s, Aunt Dorothy's two oldest children, who were entering their teenage years, were placed in the Lynchburg State Colony and sterilized. By 1963, sterilization laws were almost wholly out of use, though some remained officially on the books for many years. Virginia's state sterilization law was repealed in 1979. (7)

◆◆◆◆◆◆◆◆◆◆◆◆◆◆◆◆◆◆◆◆◆◆◆◆◆◆◆◆◆◆◆◆◆

Aunt Dorothy finally divorced Olin Kephart after he shot her in the buttocks with a shotgun and scarred her for life. She went from house to house and helped folks with chores in exchange for her room and board. She often came to Aunt Goldie's house where I hung out a lot.

Aunt Dorothy was a hypochondriac. She constantly had aches and pains. She took aspirin and anything else she could get her hands on. Larry and I would laugh at her when she would call the rescue squad and tell them she was sick. As soon as she hung up the phone, she went out on the front porch, sat on Aunt Goldie's swing, and waited for the ambulance to come for her. While she was swinging and waiting, we would ask her what was wrong with her. She always grabbed her chest and told us she had "epizulics." Other times she said she had "carbolics and flux." We rolled on the ground laughing at her. She yelled at us, "You little devils are going to be sorry someday when I die."

When the ambulance arrived, Aunt Dorothy would grab her chest and start moaning as the rescue workers brought the stretcher on the porch. She moved from the swing and onto the stretcher still holding her chest and moaning. The emergency workers loaded her into the ambulance and started on the long trip to the emergency room. However, Aunt Dorothy cried wolf one too many times. The same scenario happened repeatedly until the ambulance service refused to respond to her calls. Aunt Dorothy lived a good number of years after this time.

Uncle Shirley to the Rescue

Because of the frequent deaths of mothers in their childbearing years, there were children in Hopkins Gap who were orphaned and had no place to call home. Others could not depend on their parents for food, clothing, and shelter. These children survived by walking the road and stopping in a house around mealtime. Most families in Hopkins Gap did not lock their doors at night. A homeless child would just enter a house where they were accepted and go to bed with the children who lived there. Uncle Shirley and Aunt Ethel often told me, "We never knew how much breakfast to cook until all the kids rolled out of bed and came downstairs. We fed and sheltered a total of twenty-nine children including our nine."

The community of Hopkins Gap as a whole was friendly toward homeless or orphaned children. This is evident from studying the census data from 1910 through 1930. Families with a large number of children are listed in 1910, 1920, and 1930. A husband and wife had as many as ten children of their own as well as one or two children who were orphaned or had no home. For example, my grandfather, John Wesley Morris, died in January of

1930; the young children he left behind were living with other families according to the census recorded in June of 1930.

John Wesley Morris's brother, William Morris, and his wife, Victoria, was listed in the census with the following members of their household:

Morris, William, 53 years old–father
Victoria, 50 years old–mother
Rosie, 30 years old–daughter
Ada, 26 years old–daughter
Dodd, 20 years old–son
Everett, 18 years old–son
May, 15 years old–daughter
***Shirley Joseph,** 12 years old–nephew (John Wesley Morris's son)*
***Charlie,** 22 years old–nephew (John Wesley Morris's son)*
***James,** 17 years old–nephew (John Wesley Morris's son)*
***Richard,** 3 years old–nephew (John Wesley Morris's son)*

My oldest aunt, Aunt Zilla and her husband, John Carr opened their home to Zilla's two younger sisters.

Carr, John, age 36–father
Zilla, age 25–mother
Russell, age 9–son
Richard, age 8–son
Leonard, age 7–son
Ruth, age 5–daughter
Irene, age 4–daughter
Mildred, age 3.5–daughter
Helen, age 1.5–daughter
Kenneth, age 5 months–son
***Morris, Dorothy,** age 16–niece (John Wesley Morris's daughter)*
***Morris, Myrtle,** age 9–niece (my mother)*
(John Wesley Morris's daughter)

With eight children of their own John and Zilla, still opened their home to Zilla's orphaned sisters. A year later, in 1931, my Aunt Goldie married Robert Crawford, and they opened their home to my mother, Myrtle. She lived with them until 1940 when she married my dad, Norman Shifflett.

Again, it is obvious that it was an advantage to arrive in the "living room" bed and have many uncles, aunts, and cousins as a back-up source of care in the days when life was uncertain. Many women died in childbirth and left behind numbers of small children. A slight accident could result in death due to loss of blood or infections. The unfortunate dependent children were given homes throughout the community of Hopkins Gap.

Most homes in Hopkins Gap were open to homeless children. The two that I am most familiar with are Uncle Shirley and Aunt Ethel's home and Uncle Jim and Aunt Hazel's home. Uncle Shirley often mentioned how many children that he and Aunt Ethel had helped to raise. I asked him, "Why did you all open your doors like that?"

His answer was consistent. "Both Ethel and I were homeless kids," he said. "Ethel's mother died in the "living room" bed when Ethel was just four years old. She moved in with her sister, Hazel. Hazel was mean to Ethel, so she ended up livin' wherever she could find a place. After I found Ethel, I asked Myrtle and Norman if they would let her live with them until we got married. Ethel was fifteen when we got married. Both of us know how it feels to be wandering the roads not knowing where your next meal is coming from or if you will have clothes on your back. We always tried to do what we could."

My First Cousins

The fact that Hopkins Gap families had large numbers of children resulted in my having ninety-nine first cousins. As an adult, I think back to how I felt when my cousins from Pennsylvania came to visit. Uncle Charlie, Mom's older brother, and his wife, Madeline Dove Morris, left Hopkins Gap in the late 1930s and moved north to Pennsylvania in order to find better jobs. Uncle Charlie left first and Madeline soon followed. They were married and had five daughters.

When Uncle Charlie's family came to visit relatives in Hopkins Gap, they often stayed at Aunt Goldie and Uncle Rob's home where there were extra beds for them. We lived just across the hill from Aunt Goldie and Uncle Rob and spent a lot of time with the Pennsylvania visitors.

Two of Uncle Charlie's and Aunt Madeline's daughters.

I admired Uncle Charlie's daughters. I thought they were as pretty as you could possibly be, and they dressed better than we did, or so I thought. I did not realize that they were wearing their best clothes because they were visiting away from home. I imagined they lived in a mansion in Millersburg, Pennsylvania, where they were always warm and each one had her own room. They didn't have to go out in the cold to go to the toilet. They talked different from the way we did, and I tried to mock their accents after they left to go back home in Pennsylvania.

Other cousins had moved out of Hopkins Gap to live in Winchester, Stokesville, and Richmond, Virginia, and Baltimore, Maryland. I felt inferior to all of them mainly because of the way the others at school and at church treated those of us from Hopkins Gap. When my cousins came to visit us, we played together. Some of them were quite original in their activities. For example, my cousin, Shirley, showed me how to pee while standing up like a boy. We went behind the chicken house and practiced every time nature called, but I could never get the procedure down quite as effectively as she did.

I thought all of them were rich and went to schools where they were treated nicely. I don't recall thinking too much about whether they were treated well by the churches they attended. I was so mad about the contradictions I heard at Gospel Hill Mennonite Church that I became very indifferent to religion. The thought of church or Sunday school brought a bitter taste to my mouth, and I tried not to think about it if possible.

My numerous aunts, uncles, and ninety-nine first cousins brought many moments of joy to me. It is only in recent years that I have come to realize what a blessing they were to me. Even though some of them were more fun to be around than others, the lessons I learned from each and every one shaped my life.

PART II:

GROWING INDEPENDENT OF THE "LIVING ROOM" BED

A new baby slept in or near the "living room" bed as long as he or she was being breast-fed. As soon as she weaned the baby, the mother usually became pregnant again. At this time, the child who had enjoyed the warmth and comforts of the "living room" bed was sent to the sleeping loft to sleep.

Depending on the child's place in the birth order, he or she may have joined older brothers and sisters who already filled the beds in the sleeping loft. Joining others was better because the sleeping loft was cold, and the new arrival could be placed in between the older children to keep him or her warm.

Still, the sleeping loft was cold. Stories abound about waking up in the sleeping loft to find a nose filled with frost; waking up to a frozen chamber pot–described as "piss sickles" by some–or waking up to a skiff of snow that had blown in the cracks of the wall to blanket the top of the covers.

While in the sleeping loft, children were exposed to childhood diseases such as mumps, measles, and whooping cough. They also experienced cuts, bruises, and broken bones. During recovery, parents placed children back in the "living room" bed where they received full attention, special foods, and wonderful care from their mothers and older brothers and sisters. Children who had many siblings found these times very meaningful. Although pain and discomfort were the reasons they had been placed in the "living room" bed, children were so comforted by the attention that many spoke of "not minding the measles at all because I felt so good being back in the 'living room" bed."

Once a child entered the sleeping loft with the older children, it was not long before he or she was expected to start helping with chores around the house. The chores were simple at first and included such things as going to the hen house with Momma to help gather the eggs, helping pull weeds in the garden, or swatting flies in the house. All children were expected to contribute to "earn their keep," as my mom always said. The little jobs typically followed along gender lines with the girls helping the mother and the boys helping the father. All jobs were designed to prepare children for their future roles as husband and wife.

Chapter 8

Graduating to the Sleeping Loft

"Maturity is a bitter disappointment for which no remedy exists, unless laughter can be said to remedy anything."

Thomas Edison

Once a mother weaned a young child from the breast, usually because a new baby was on the way, she sent him or her out of the "living room" bed and up to the sleeping loft to sleep with the older brothers and sisters. The slow and reluctant walk up the rickety stairs was the beginning of the most difficult part of a child's life. At the same time, it was the beginning of separation from the parents and becoming a member of the older children.

The sleeping loft was located in the upper level of the house, usually above the living room. It had a lower ceiling than the living room. The ceiling consisted of the rafters covered by the roof. There was no insulation, and the wind often carried snow in through the cracks between the roof and the wall. Children accessed the sleeping loft by a narrow stairway from the living room. In some houses with no second floor, the older children slept in one room that was isolated from the living room and kitchen stove; therefore, it was very cold in the winter.

Life was not easy for the young child in the sleeping loft. The beds were already crowded with older brothers and sisters, and they resented a new intruder. Sometimes the new arrival ended up on the coldest side of the bed away from the stovepipe. Many times the sleeping child lost the covers to older bedfellows who pulled them off during the night.

Grandpa Austin and Grandma Molly Shifflett lived in a house in Hopkins Gap. It had a typical sleeping loft.

"My older sisters put me in between them in the bed. They thought they were keeping me warm, but the covers didn't stay down on me and let cold air in. I nearly froze to death," said Peggy, the youngest of ten children. She was born in a "living room" bed and grew up in the mountains of Patrick County, Virginia.

The furnishings in the sleeping loft were sparse and consisted of homemade beds and a chamber pot. Depending on the size of the loft and the number of children, there were two or three beds–one for the boys and one for the girls, and possibly a third for extra girls or boys.

However, if the family could afford only one bed or the space didn't allow two beds, the boys slept at the bottom of the bed and the girls at the top. This resulted in having toes poked in your mouth and nose, being kicked in whatever body part was in the way, and smelling dirty feet all night. There were no closets for hanging clothing. Clothes hung on nails in the wall or from a wire strung from the rafters.

"We had two beds up there–one for the boys and one for us girls. When the boys got a little older, Momma moved them downstairs in a cold room just off the living room," Peggy said of the sleeping loft in her small log home.

"Our beds were homemade with a solid wood head board and a solid wood platform to lie on. Daddy cut down some small trees and used the trunks for bedposts. He laid the trunks down on the ground and nailed boards across them for the headboard. Then he nailed boards across two longer tree trunks for the part we slept on. He nailed shorter tree trunks under the corners of the platform for the bed legs then attached the head board," Peggy said.

Straw Ticks

Straw ticks were large cotton bags that were stuffed with straw, a by-product of threshing the grain out of wheat and barley. Straw ticks were laid on top of the wooden platform part of the bed, and the children slept on top of them.

When children urinated on the straw tick, it soaked through. The straw tick did not fully dry before the next bedtime. The children had to sleep in a damp bed. After a few nights, the smell of urine was overwhelming.

Peggy said, "We slept on the straw ticks. Mama tried to find time to change the straw in our ticks once a month. The only time I was ever warm in the winter was when Momma had stuffed the ticks with fresh straw. I could wiggle down in the new straw. I looked forward to going to bed on the first night after she changed the straw because the new straw made the bed fluffy and fresh smelling. I slept warmer on those nights with new straw. Once the straw settled down, I was just lying on the flat board. I slept in between two older sisters, and

Here we see two young people at the barn with the straw tick as they fill it up with fresh straw.

that's probably the reason I'm here today. Once in a while I would cry and Momma would let me go down stairs and sleep with her in the warm 'living room' bed."

Unfortunately, the fresh straw did not remain so for long, Peggy said. "It was too cold to get up and use the pot," she explained. "Most of the time our beds were damp and pretty smelly." Sometimes children tried hard to hold their urine all night because the covers on top of them weighed them down to where they could barely move. This simply didn't work because sleep brought on a relaxing of muscles, and they ended up sleeping in their own puddles as well as the puddles of their sleeping mates.

The Chamber Pot or "Slop Jar"

There were no indoor bathrooms, so nighttime toileting needs were met with a chamber pot or an old bucket. Sometimes this facility was humorously called the "slop jar" or "thunder mug." We had a slop jar in our upstairs when I was growing up. My sister and I were expected to carry the slop jar down the stairs each morning and empty it. Because the lid to the slop jar had been lost years before, I found that to be a very smelly and offensive chore and often managed to forget it when it was my turn. Sometimes Mom discovered my forgetfulness by the smell that wafted down the stairs later in the day. It was not unheard of at our house for the slop jar to get so full Mom had to take a little tub upstairs and gently set the pot into the tub so the contents wouldn't splash out on the floor.

My daddy usually relieved himself off the back porch before he went to bed each night. However, he sometimes had to use the chamber pot during the night. Mom cursed my daddy when that happened. "He stands there and keeps on pissin' in the slop jar until he runs it over. He has never carried this stinkin' thing out of here–not once," she said.

One time my sister was carrying the slop jar down the stairs when she tripped over something. She and the slop jar went crashing all the way to the bottom. She screamed with pain and fear as Mom came running to find the contents of the slop jar dripping off the edges of the steps. We had a closet under the stairs. The slop jar contents dripped into the closet and forced a major cleaning and washing. Nobody thought that accident was funny as we all were slapped and made to help with the clean up.

In the dead of winter, we would awaken to find the contents of the slop jar frozen solid. Because the slop jar would not expand, the frozen chunk bulged up in the middle and we called it by various names such as a "piss berg" or "piss sickles." We had to carry the slop jar downstairs and pour hot water in it to empty the contents. After the slop jar was empty and rinsed out, Mom handed us a bottle of concentrated liquid Lysol. We dribbled a little of it in the bottom of the slop jar and took it back upstairs for the next night.

◆◆◆◆◆◆◆◆◆◆◆◆◆◆◆◆◆◆◆◆◆◆◆◆◆◆◆◆◆◆◆◆◆

Searchin' for a Dry Bed . . .

My first cousin, Betty, grew up with nine brothers and sisters. She was Uncle Shirley and Aunt Ethel's third child. Uncle Shirley and Aunt Ethel opened their doors to many of the homeless children in Hopkins Gap. Betty told me, "Me and Mom counted up one day not long ago. We figured that, countin' us kids, Mom and Dad helped to raise twenty-nine children."

Betty was a constant victim of younger children peeing on her at night. With an anger that has endured over her sixty-plus years, she said, "Many nights I woke up soakin' wet because one of my younger brothers or sisters had pissed on me. Often it was one of the kids that just stayed at our house. You never knew who you were goin' to wake up with in the morning. I remember one particular night when I woke up and my nightclothes were soakin' wet with piss. I got out of bed and put on dry clothes and then I went searchin' for a dry bed. I was fumblin' around in the dark feeling in all the beds for one that was dry, and Dad heard me from downstairs."

Her father yelled at her and asked her what she was doing out of bed. When she told him she was looking for a dry place to sleep, he said, "If you fall down the steps while you are lookin' for a dry bed, I am goin' to whip your ass on top of it."

As fate would have it, she did indeed fall down the steps. "Dad came runnin' to the bottom of the steps, picked me up, and beat my ass until it burned like fire," Betty said. "He carried me up the steps and threw me into a bed and said, 'There now, I found you a dry bed.' It turns out that bed had been pissed in too, but I was afraid to move again."

◆◆◆◆◆◆◆◆◆◆◆◆◆◆◆◆◆◆◆◆◆◆◆◆◆◆◆◆◆◆◆◆◆◆◆◆◆◆

Pat, from Franklin County, Virginia, was the youngest of ten children. When she was cast out of the "living room" bed, she graduated to an ice-cold sleeping room. "I could never keep any covers on me even though Momma told my older sisters to put me in the middle of the bed so I would stay warm," Pat said. "They put me in the middle but they were bigger than I was and their bodies kept the covers up off of me. One night, I got so cold I jumped out of bed and ran to my brother's bed. I jumped in and clung to his back with my arms around his neck. He woke up and asked me if I had a problem and I said I was freezin' to death. He let me stay in bed with him until morning."

The Stove Pipe

My cousins in Hopkins Gap gave testimony to the many challenges of life in the sleeping loft. In the living room, you most always found a woodstove that heated the living room. The stovepipe ran through the ceiling and through the sleeping loft on its way out of the roof. Some heat inevitably reached the sleeping loft; but it was so unevenly distributed that its usefulness was far surpassed by the dangers of an exposed metal pipe. The problem with the stovepipe heat was that it kept the area immediately around the pipe very hot, but the heat never spread throughout the loft. The bare metal pipe had to be avoided by the children sleeping up there for fear of burns. If a child rose to use the chamber pot and bumped an arm or leg against the bare stovepipe, a severe burn could result and the original reason to getting out of bed was forgotten or eliminated by loss of bladder control.

"See this scar?" said one of my cousins as she displayed a mark on her upper arm. "I got really bad burns when I got out of bed to use the pot. I was scared to get out and use the pot any more so I just peed in the bed when I couldn't hold it 'til morning. The worst part was that the stovepipe didn't really heat the loft. It was boilin' hot if you slept beside the stovepipe, but two feet away a body could have froze to death. When you was close to the pipe, one side of your body was scorchin' and the other side freezin'. It was miserable in the winter and hotter than hell in the summer."

Comforters

The children in the sleeping loft covered themselves with handmade comforters. Comforters were different from Appalachian Mountain quilts. They were far less artful, strictly utilitarian, and very heavy. When the wind was howling outside, my sister and I had as many as four comforters on top of us. There was no turning over or moving with all that weight.

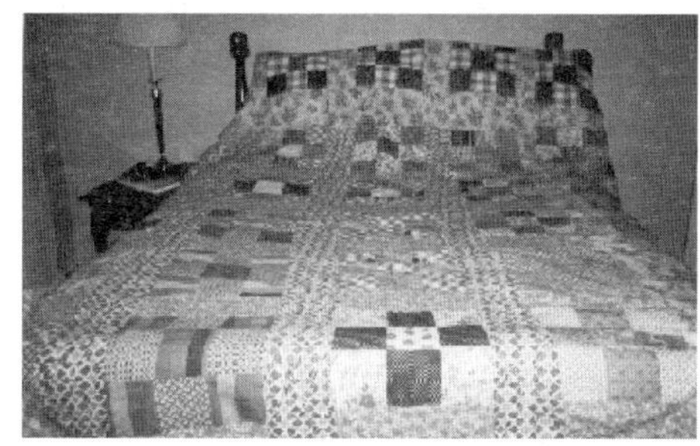

This is one of Mom's comforters that she made from scraps of feed sacks that she had sewn dresses and shirts for us to wear.

Unfortunately, even with all that cover, we still froze during the coldest nights.

The tops of the comforters were made with scraps of material from old clothing or scraps from the sewing basket after dresses, skirts, and shirts were created. The bottoms of the comforters consisted of a solid colored piece of material. This was usually made by sewing together four cotton flour or feed sacks.

This is a picture of a quilt–much more complicated in the number of stitches–not a practical way to keep a lot of children warm because of the time involved in making a quilt.

◆◆◆◆◆◆◆◆◆◆◆◆◆◆◆◆◆◆◆◆◆◆◆◆◆◆◆◆◆◆◆◆◆

Feed Sacks . . .

Prior to 1929, cotton was an expensive fabric. The bottom fell out of the cotton market during the Great Depression and then cotton was replaced with rayon as the preferred cloth for clothing. Manufacturers of livestock feed had been using boxes and barrels to ship their products; but, with the availability of inexpensive cotton cloth, boxes and barrels were

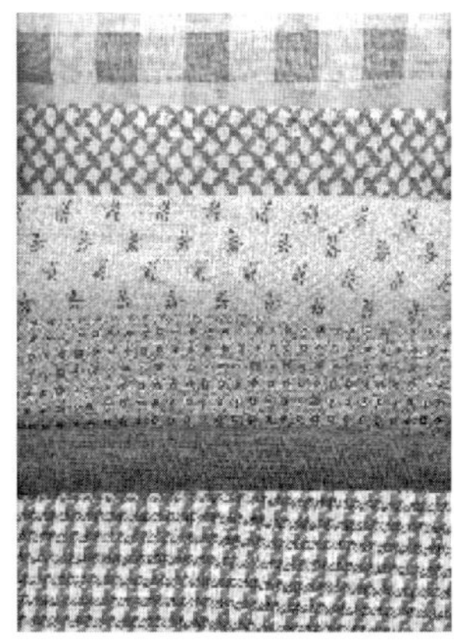

Shown here is a stack of Mom's feed sacks and a close up of a feed sack design. When Mom died, we discovered three barrels of feed sacks in an upstairs room. They were all washed ironed and neatly folded away for her future sewing projects.

replaced with cotton sacks. The cotton sacks were originally white with the product name stamped on them.

Farmwomen, who were very frugal, bleached the product name out of the white sacks and used them to sew underwear, women's slips, pillowcases, and other hand-sewn items. By the late 1930s, manufacturers figured out that they would sell more of their products if they used solid-colored sacks. Then manufacturers hired artists to design prints for their sacks. With printed feed sacks and flour bags, farmwomen took thriftiness to new heights of creativity, transforming the humble bags into dresses, underwear, towels, curtains, quilts, sewing machine covers, and other household necessities.

My brother, Larry, wearing a shirt made of feed sacks with a cowboy and Indian print on it.

I was born in 1941. For the first fourteen years of my life, my mother sewed most of my dresses and all of my underwear from feed sacks. She saved every leftover scrap of feed sackcloth from dress making to make comforter tops. All of my brothers and my sister wore feed sack clothes. Some of the feed sacks were printed with cowboys and horses, especially for boys clothing. Mom would be very creative and would add different details to each item of clothing. Some were sleeveless. Others had little puffy fifties sleeves or self collars or contrasting solid collars, and most of

This is Pat, from Franklin County, wearing a dress that her mother made from feed sacks and trimmed in rickrack. Scraps from this dress ended up in the comforters that kept Pat warm in the cold winters.

them had at least some rickrack for decoration. My schoolmates teased me about my feed-sack dresses, and I longed for store-bought dresses. Now I wish I had kept those feed-sack dresses.

◆◆◆◆◆◆◆◆◆◆◆◆◆◆◆◆◆◆◆◆◆◆◆◆◆◆◆◆◆◆◆◆◆

In the early days, the comforter bottom was laid out across a bed and then lined with a thick layer of sheep wool. Later on, during the 1950s and 1960s, the comfort maker was able to buy rolls of cotton batting at five and dime stores such as Woolworth. The batting was rolled out onto the comforter bottom. The patched top of the comforter was spread over the top of the batting. The comfort maker then lapped the bottom up over the patched top by about one inch and sewed the bottom to the patched top leaving about a one inch border around the outside of the comforter.

With the comforter still lying on the bed, the comfort maker took cotton twine string and stitched the top and bottom together to prevent the wool or the batting from shifting inside the comforter. These stitches were about twelve inches apart.

The twine string was stitched in by pushing the needle through the patched top of the comforter and then pushing it back through from the comforter bottom to the patched top. The twine string was snipped off, leaving two pieces of string on the patched top. These strings were about two inches long and were tied into a knot; thus holding the patched top and the bottom together and, at the same time, securing the wool or batting inside the comforter.

These were either handed down from grandmothers or made by mothers during the long winter months when the gardening and canning season was over. My mom had comforters that Grandma Molly gave her when she first married; but she used the long winter evenings to make her own comforters. Her comforters were always clean and if they tore, she immediately patched them. I always felt safe and secure sleeping under Mom's comforters.

My sister and I played a game with the patched comforter

top. We tried to see who could identify the pieces that made up the patched top. We found pieces of our own school dresses and skirts, our brothers' shirts, Mom's aprons, and Dad's work clothes.

Dad always wore his pants out on the front of the legs by lifting and dumping sacks of feed mix into the mixer at Rockingham Milling Company where he worked. Mom never wasted anything, so she used the backs of the pants legs and any other salvageable part to add to her patched comforter tops.

Mom liked to dye her cotton sacks that she used for comforter bottoms. She bought her dye in powder form, so it was easy to dye her cloth. Mom always picked a dominant color from her patched comforter top and dyed the comforter bottom to match it. The edge of the comforter bottom that bordered the comforter top always looked nice with the multi-colored patches of cloth. Folks used the most colorful comforters on the "living room" bed because this bed was exposed to all who visited in the home.

◆◆◆◆◆◆◆◆◆◆◆◆◆◆◆◆◆◆◆◆◆◆◆◆◆◆◆◆◆◆◆◆◆◆

Grandma Mary Lam Morris' Comforters . . .

One of my favorite times with Mom was when she was making comforters during the long winter evenings. As she worked on her comforters, she told me stories of her mother and how she made quilts. She said, "I was only five years old when Mom died, but my older sisters told me a lot about Mom. She didn't have these cotton bats like I buy. She gathered sheep wool from the barbed wire fences. The sheep brushed their sides or scratched themselves against the barbs on the wire. When their wool was long and ready to shear, they left pretty large chunks of wool."

My grandmother would walk along the fencerows to collect chunks of wool. When she had enough, she cleaned the wool, made a comforter top and bottom, and stuffed it with the wool. "There was nothing warmer than a comforter filled with sheep wool. The colder the weather got outside, the warmer that comforter felt," my mother said.

Mom went on to describe how Grandma Mary used natural things to dye her quilt bottoms. "Mom loved colors. She always wore bright-colored calico dresses and aprons. Instead of just putting a white cotton bottom on her comforters, she gathered flowers, roots, and other things to dye her cotton sacks. She collected flower blooms and wild berries. She had to get them when they were at their peak of color. Berries had to be dead ripe," she said.

Mom remembered a few of the natural plants that Grandma Mary used to make her dyes. She used bloodroot or sassafras leaves for shades of orange. She used oak bark, sumac leaves, or acorns for shades of brown. Blue or purple dyes were made from mulberries, blackberries, or elderberries. Dandelion root, pokeweed berries, and beets made a red dye. "I do remember Stella (Mom's sister) telling me that Mom used vinegar to hold the colors she made with plants and salt to fix the colors she made with berries. I can't remember how she mixed all the stuff," Mom added.

◆◆◆◆◆◆◆◆◆◆◆◆◆◆◆◆◆◆◆◆◆◆◆◆◆◆◆◆◆◆◆◆◆◆◆◆

One evening made me appreciate Mom's comforters. I was about ten or eleven years old. Dad put us all in the car so we could visit Aunt Stella and Uncle Clarence. We didn't visit them very often because Stella was much older than Mom, and they were not very close. She had married young and moved away before the death of Grandma Mary. Aunt Stella and Uncle Clarence had nine or ten children. They lived in a typical mountain house with a sleeping loft above the living room.

During the evening, I went up into the sleeping loft to play with my cousins. I saw their beds. The comforters were torn and dirty, and I felt sorry for them because they had to sleep under those awful comforters. When we returned home and went to bed, I cried myself to sleep because my cousins were sleeping under those comforters. For some reason, I have never forgotten that evening. Perhaps it was the beginning of my great appreciation for Mom.

Moving from the warm "living room" bed to the sleeping loft was a life-changing event for children. This simple move from one bed to another initiated a new phase of life–the first step to maturity. The new phase included growing up physically and becoming a productive member of the community. The "living room" bed remained in the corner of the living room but its purpose changed from a birthing bed to a healing bed for the children who had just left it to sleep in the cold loft.

Chapter 9

Surviving Childhood Illnesses

"A man is wise with the wisdom of his time only, and ignorant with its ignorance"

Henry David Thoreau

Returning to the Living Room Bed

One of the sad things about being one child in a household of many children was that mothers and daddies did not have enough time to give each child the attention he or she needed. However, parents did pay attention to sickness or injury; thus, some children didn't mind being sick at all.

Returning to the "living room" bed and receiving special attention lessened the pain of measles, mumps, chicken pox, and injuries. Manila, a woman from Floyd County, Virginia, told me, "I didn't mind the measles at all. Momma put me in the living room bed, and covered me up with comforters. Daddy got the measles at the same time I did, so he got in beside me, and we drank hot lemonade with a teaspoon of moonshine in it."

Nadine, a Patrick County, Virginia, woman said, "When I had the flu, Grandma Scott put me in the living room bed. She had a fire in the fireplace. She brought me chicken soup. I never have felt so warm, so loved, and as protected as I did that time.

I still think about how wonderful I felt in that warm bed even though I had the flu."

I had a similar experience with the flu. We didn't always have a bed in the living room because Mom didn't want Dad to take naps on it and mess it up. However, when I became sick, Mom moved a bed next to the living room stove. She put me in the bed. She made special food and frequently checked my temperature by putting her lips on my forehead. I felt very special as that was one of my few moments with Mom's full attention.

Methods of Treatment

In my experiences with childhood illnesses and other maladies such as cuts and beestings, I noted two ways that Grandma Molly and Mom handled these situations. One was with sympathetic and homeopathic rituals to prevent and cure certain conditions. The other was gathering, mixing, brewing, or otherwise preparing teas, poultices, or pills as preventions or treatments. They either applied these items directly to the condition or made the afflicted child ingest them.

The sympathetic and homeopathic rituals were very strange, but mostly not painful. I witnessed one that may have been painful. My cousin, who had whooping cough, endured a trip through the grain hopper at the gristmill as a cure. His parents stuck him in the hopper, where he flopped around and banged against the sides for a few minutes. When he came out, he was covered with grain dust. As I look back on this, I think the dust may have made his whooping cough worse; however, what do I know about magic?

The treatments that Mom or Grandma Molly applied or forced us to ingest were the worst. It seemed to me that Grandma Molly had a use for every type of animal feces. She used cow manure for blemishes; sheep manure for measles; hog manure for mumps; the white part of chicken manure for stomachache; and cat manure for whatever the other treatments could not cure.

Luckily for me and my siblings, Mom did not allow Grandma Molly to use manure cures on us.

Diagnosis, Treatment, and Prevention

Mountain mothers and grandmothers carried most of their "medical" information around in their heads, and they constantly watched the children for signs of sickness. They also tried hard to prevent illness. As my childhood years went by, Mom turned to sources other than Grandma Molly for her preventatives and cures. I am not saying she ignored Grandma Molly; however, she did expand her search to the unscientific medical advice of those who were trying to sell patent medicines.

She frequently read about various illnesses and their preventions in the *Grit* paper. *Grit* was a weekly newspaper popular in rural areas throughout the United States during much of the twentieth century. Once, she read a short piece on anemia and immediately decided I was lazy because I had anemia. While it is possible that I was anemic at one point in my life, with my mother, treatment never stopped. She bought big bottles of SSS tonic. SSS tonic was advertised on the back cover of her *True Confessions* magazine–the only magazine she ever read or allowed in the house without a lot of fuss. She liked the *Grit* paper; but she hated the books that Dad brought home.

Dad loved to read and devoured any books loaned to him or newspapers he could get his hands on. He spread them out on the dining room table as he read every word. Dad never threw a newspaper away, because he could always go back and read them again. His piles of papers and books angered Mom because she had to move them to put a meal on the table.

Mom looked forward to her new *True Confessions,* which came in the mail once a month. She told me that she had been reading them since she was a teenager. "I taught myself to read by reading the love stories," she said. Mom had dropped out of school in the fifth grade. As I think back on her devotion to the magazine, I wonder if she liked the love stories or if she liked the advertisements for various patent medicines she could try on me.

Mom administered SSS tonic to me by the tablespoon. The morning after she received the medicine in the mail, she pulled the bottle down off the shelf, poured me three tablespoons of it, and handed me the glass. The foul liquid tasted like concentrated blood that had been aged for several days. Even today, I shudder as I think of it. After several doses, I said to her, "Mom, please mix this stuff with something good. It tastes awful."

"All right," she said. "Go to the cellar and get me a can of grape juice." I loved the grape juice that Mom and Aunt Goldie canned each September. They spent several days picking and processing white grapes and blue Concord grapes that grew on arbors under Aunt Goldie's kitchen window. That juice was wonderful, but when my mother mixed it with SSS tonic, the delicious flavor disappeared. The foul tonic wiped out the taste. I wasn't able to get it past my nose so I could swallow it. I tried holding my nose shut–didn't help–nothing worked. I believed I suffered more by taking the medicine than I would have with a bad case of anemia.

One morning I had a bright idea. "I think I could drink this stuff in coffee." I said to Mom. I had been begging for coffee for some months.

"You are too young to drink coffee; but, if it will get this medicine in you, I'll give you some," she replied.

Mom poured the three tablespoons in a coffee cup and poured coffee on top of it. She added milk. I tried to drink the mixture, but again, the taste of coffee disappeared when Mom mixed the SSS tonic in with it. Finally, I told Mom, "I think I could drink the tonic if I went outside in the fresh air." She agreed, and mixed the coffee and SSS tonic so I could take it outside. I poured the mixture in the flowerbed by the kitchen door, and continued to do that every day.

Over time, the flowers seemed to grow taller, and I regretted that I had not benefited myself from SSS tonic. After she had used two bottles, Mom said, "I don't think that SSS tonic is helping with your anemia. You're still pale and skinny. I can read the Bible through your ribs. I saw a new tonic in *True Confessions* that I'm gonna order for you. It's called Geritol." It didn't taste one bit better than the SSS tonic, and it too became food for the flowers.

◆◆◆◆◆◆◆◆◆◆◆◆◆◆◆◆◆◆◆◆◆◆◆◆◆◆◆◆◆◆◆◆◆

Paregoric . . .

How many remember the bottle of paregoric that moms pulled off the highest shelf and administered by the spoonful? Mothers used this common household remedy in the eighteenth and nineteenth centuries, when it was widely used to calm fretful children. The medicine also calmed diarrhea and incessant coughing in adults and children; it could be purchased over the counter at any drugstore. Its use declined in the twentieth century as governments regulated it. The regulation consisted of having the customer sign their name in a book when they purchased paregoric.

The principal active ingredient in paregoric was powdered opium. Other ingredients included camphor and anise oil. The anise oil gave paregoric a good flavor so it wasn't hard to swallow. The soothing opium offered deep sleep. (8) Both of these effects were useful for mothers who were busy with household chores and many children. They gave a crying baby a dose of paregoric, rocked him to sleep in the "big rocker," and then laid him on the "living room" bed for a long nap.

I recall Mom talking about the adults who had purchased so much paregoric that the drug store wouldn't sell it to them anymore. They had become addicted. They often came to her and asked her to purchase paregoric for them. She obliged until her kindness threatened her own access to the drug.

◆◆◆◆◆◆◆◆◆◆◆◆◆◆◆◆◆◆◆◆◆◆◆◆◆◆◆◆◆◆◆◆◆

I guess the worst medicine we were given was asafetida, though luckily, I didn't have to eat or drink it. Asafetida was supposed to ward off the sicknesses that were common in the winter. Grandma Molly said it kept away evil spirits and witches so they couldn't put a spell on you. The odor of asafetida was enough to keep anything or anybody at a far distance.

Asafetida came in cakes that looked a little like a cake of chewing tobacco. Drugstores carried it in those days. Mothers cut a small chunk off the cake, placed in a little cloth bag, and tied it around a child's neck. When I went to first grade, some of the children who rode my school bus had these little bags on strings around their necks from September until March.

Certain children seemed to have more health problems than others did. My brother, Larry, was one of them. He liked to play in the dirt, and he liked to eat it too. When he was two or three years old, he took a spoon out into the yard and ate dirt by the spoonful. More than one time Mom caught him with his mouth full of dirt. She had to dig it out of his jaws and throat with her finger.

If you can imagine what might have been in that dirt, then you must have grown up or visited rural areas. Our chickens roamed free, and of course, they pecked around in the dirt. When they needed to poop, they turned their tail end down toward the ground and squirted wherever they happened to be at the time.

Cats and dogs also ran free. There was no such thing as a litter box for cats or a leash for walking dogs to the appropriate place for their bathroom activities. Mom often stated with her threatening voice, "If I catch any of you bringing a cat in the house, I am going to rub your nose in their mess." Occasionally the cows found their way through the fence and walked through the back yard on the way to eat up the garden. Without further comment, I think we can imagine the type of things Larry was ingesting with each spoonful of dirt. Not long after his dirt-for-lunch experiences, Larry ran screaming into the house. "What's wrong?"

Mom asked, frantic. Larry pointed to his pants. Mom picked him up and saw a huge roundworm crawling around in his underwear. It had managed to escape from the large wriggly nest of fellow worms that lived in his intestine.

Panic stricken, Mom went next door to Pop May's house to use the community telephone. She called my dad at work and told him what she had found. "When I get home from work, we'll drive over to the Gap to see what Grandma Molly can do," Dad told her. Mom had no choice since she couldn't drive a car.

When we arrived at Grandma Molly's house, she laughed at Mom for getting so scared. "Most kids who play outdoors get worms," she chuckled. "Here, let me go out along the garden fence and get you some worm weed. We'll chop it up and put it in his food."

Grandma Molly wasn't gone long. She returned with some dark green weed tops in her hand. She chopped them up with a sharp knife and gave them to Mom in a little cloth bag with a drawstring. "Put about a half of a teaspoon in his breakfast tomorrow morning," she advised.

Mom did what Grandma Molly said, but she still worried that more worms might crawl out of her little son. "We are taking Larry to the doctor on Saturday. I don't care what you say," she told Dad. "The idea of worms like the one I saw alivin' in his stomach is more than I can stand. Why no wonder he cries with a belly ache all the time." The doctor gave Mom medicine that cured Larry's worms, but that wasn't the only time she found worms in his underwear. He just seemed to love the dirt in the back yard.

Not surprisingly, other children cried with the stomachache. Their parents treated them with turpentine mixed with sugar. "I drank so much turpentine; I should be a Sequoia or a loblolly pine tree," Peggy, who grew up in the mountains of Patrick County, Virginia, told me. "Momma had me to drink the turpentine and sugar and put me in the "living room" bed. She warmed her flat iron on the stove, wrapped it up in a rag, and placed it on my stomach."

When that didn't help, Peggy, who was twelve years old, went to the doctor. That day she also visited the Ben Franklin Store in Rocky Mount. It was a first time for both events. "The doctor sent me home with medicine for my worms, and he also gave Momma some worm medicine for my pet cats. Pretty soon my stomachache was gone and never came back," Peggy said.

As I questioned people all up and down the Appalachians, from Grayson County to Mathias, West Virginia, I found some maladies that were familiar only to those who grew up in Hopkins Gap. For example, *livergrown* was one illness that attacked little babies between one and three months old in Hopkins Gap. Some folks thought *livergrown* was really what old folks called pneumonia. That made sense because it was usually a problem in the winter months. Folks believed that riding a newborn baby in a buggy over a bumpy road, or riding a child on horseback so it was being bumped up and down and breathing cold air, caused *livergrown*. They thought the liver attached itself to the ribs, which caused the baby to be unable to swallow milk or to cry in more than a whimper. Mom told me, "They got so sore they could hardly breathe. They just laid and grunted for their breath."

As Grandma Molly grew older, she passed much of her knowledge down to Mom. This was the first change is medical practices in Hopkins Gap. According to area folklore, Grandma Molly had the knowledge of "medicine" because she was born after the death of her father. In her "medical" practices, she included saying the "words" after she performed each ritual. For example, she treated a child for some condition they had, and then she repeated three times in Pennsylvania Dutch, "In the name of the Father, the Son, and the Holy Ghost."

Mom acquired her own "medical knowledge" by observing Grandma Molly. When she returned home from observing, she said, "I don't think them words have anything to do with the curing. I'm gonna try it myself, and I don't even know the words."

Because she didn't understand Pennsylvania Dutch, she dropped the "words" from her treatments. After that, I remember Mom curing many babies of *livergrown*. My cousins from Hopkins Gap would drive up in front of the house and climb out of the car with their newborn babies. As soon as they were inside, Mom would begin her diagnosis. She lifted the baby from its mother's arms and laid it on a blanket on the dining room table. She pushed gently on its chest." Is she sucking the bottle?" she asked. If the mother answered no, Mom would make a clucking noise with her tongue, "Tsk, tsk, tsk." Then she would ask, "Can she cry?"

If the mother answered no, Mom had only one more question to ask before her diagnosis of *livergrown* was complete. "Has anybody been bouncin' this baby in the cold air?"

The mother would think hard. "Well yes. Her daddy was throwing her up in the air in front of the kitchen door. I told him to stop, but he said he was just playin' with her," she would say.

"Well," Mom would reply. "I'm sure it's *livergrown*. If you want me to grease her, I'll do it. Greasin' her can't hurt nothin' even if it ain't *livergrown*."

The mother always answered, "Okay, you go ahead and grease her."

Mom mixed up hog lard and camphor in a bowl and then she rubbed it on the baby's chest. She then put her hands around the baby's chest with her fingers on the back of the ribcage. She placed her thumbs side by side on the front of the baby's chest and pressed down. She moved her thumbs down over the sternum and around the edges of the rib cage. She pressed so hard that the rib cage stood well above her thumbs as she moved them around the edges.

The baby whimpered as Mom pressed her thumbs deeper into its abdomen. She did this nine times on the front, then turned the baby over and did it nine times on the back. She explained as she rubbed, "You know, Grandma Molly always said the words when she cured for *livergrown*. I don't say the words. I really don't believe in the words. I think it is the grease and rubbing that really helps."

I thought Mom would crush the baby's chest. She really squeezed hard. I glanced at the mother's face. It was screwed up as if she felt the pain of her newborn baby.

"Don't that hurt?" she asked.

"Yeah, it probably does, but I have to rub hard to loosen her liver from her ribs," Mom assured her.

When the ritual was over, Mom wrapped the baby in its blanket, "Here," she told the mother, "set down in the "big rocker" and give her some milk." Without fail, the baby would start nursing, and in a few minutes, fall fast asleep. The mother would then lay the baby on the "living room" bed.

"Myrt, what do I owe you?" the relieved mother would ask.

"Not a thing," Mom always answered. "You can stay a while and let the baby sleep; you just bring her back if she gets to feelin' bad again."

Grandma Molly kept an eye on all the children in Hopkins Gap. When we went near her, she checked our fingers for warts, punched around in our stomachs to see if we had worms, or pulled up our shirts and looked for "tetter," which was her name for eczema. If she found a wart, she would, without warning, spit a glob of snuff saliva on it. She did that to me one time, and made me so mad I cried. I wanted to kill her, but I knew better. When I cried, she laughed and said, "If it don't make ya mad, the treatment don't work." Sure enough, the wart was gone in a few weeks.

Warnie, my youngest brother, told a story of Grandma Molly pulling up his shirt and discovering a spot of "tetter." She spit snuff saliva in both of her hands, rubbed them together, and then rubbed her hands on his back. He squirmed and cried as he tried to escape her clutches. She laughed, "It's gotta make ya mad or it don't work," she said to him. Warnie swears that his "tetter" disappeared in no time.

One of Grandma Molly's major jobs was to make sure

children were growing properly. Her test for this was to grab a handful of flesh on the back of the arm. She squeezed on it and made an immediate diagnosis. If she said, "You're doin' good," it was a lucky day for you.

Grandma Molly found many children who were not growing like she thought they should. Several of my cousins reported that Grandma Molly measured them. My cousin, Betty recently told me that she was measured. Her description followed the exact procedure that I went through myself at the hands of Grandma Molly. I was four years old when Grandma grabbed my upper arm and gave it a squeeze. "Your flesh is loose from your bone," she said. "You have *undergrowth*." Then she went and found Mom. "This kid's got *undergrowth*. You bring her over here in the next new moon so I can measure her," she told her.

Without questioning Grandma Molly's diagnosis, Mom said, "Okay. I'll check the almanac and see when the moon is new."

A few weeks later, I found myself stripped naked and standing in the middle of Grandma Molly's kitchen table. She held a red string. First, she measured my foot. "If her body is not more than seven times the length of her foot, she has *undergrowth* for sure," she explained to Mom. Then she held the string at the spot that was equal to seven times the length of my foot, and measured from the crown of my head to my heel. She found that I was slightly shorter than seven times the length of my foot. "Well," she announced, "this kid has *undergrowth*. I'll go ahead and treat her since it is the new moon, but she needs to be measured two more times in the next two new moons."

"What difference does the new moon make?" Mom asked.

"If you want something to grow, you treat it when the moon is increasing in size. That's why I tell you and Norman to plant your garden in the new moon," Grandma Molly patiently explained.

Mom accepted that explanation from Grandma Molly, as she usually did, without question.

Grandma Molly tied the red string in a knot and laid it in

a circle on the kitchen table. She said to me, "Now, you step over into that circle." I did as I was told. She picked the string up from the table and pulled it up over my head, which was the direction of growth. She mumbled words in Pennsylvania Dutch. I assume they were, "In the name of the Father, the Son, and the Holy Ghost." She pulled the string up over my body two more times, followed by the words. Then she balled the string up, walked to her pie safe, and placed the string in a corner of the top drawer. She took her almanac off the wall where it hung just above the water bucket. She opened it to the following month and told Mom, "You bring her back over here again in the new moon."

The following month, Grandma Molly repeated the same ritual. She gave me the final treatment a month later. After the third treatment, she balled the red string up in her hand. She asked me to get down off the table so Mom could help me put my clothes on. When I was dressed, she said, "Now come outside with me and I will show you something." She went out the door, crossed the porch, and stopped at the corner of the house. She explained, "I am going to bury this string here at the corner of the house where the rain drips off the roof. By the time the string is rotted, you'll be growin' again like you're s'posed to." We went back into the house and nothing more was said about *undergrowth*.

The children growing up along the Appalachian Mountains didn't receive "baby shots" to protect them from the measles, mumps, and chicken pox. They caught all of the childhood diseases and had to suffer the consequences. Many times the treatments were worse than the illness. Take for example, the measles. One child would break out with the measles and one by one, the whole bunch of children had them. One by one, each sick child was assigned to the "living room" bed until the fever subsided.

◆◆◆◆◆◆◆◆◆◆◆◆◆◆◆◆◆◆◆◆◆◆◆◆◆◆◆◆◆◆◆◆◆

Measles . . .

There are officially two kinds of measles: Rubeola and Rubella. Rubeola measles lasted for three days. They were called "ordinary" measles and they could cause fever, cough, "pink eye," and a red bumpy rash. The rash appeared inside the cheeks, then started at the hairline and spread over the whole body. Before immunization, measles appeared about every two years during the winter and spring months. Mothers were almost happy when measles appeared and would purposefully expose their children so they could be prepared and "get it over with." Mothers believed they needed to keep their sick children warm and in a dark room, so they placed the child with measles in the "living room" bed by the stove. They covered the windows with dark blankets or comforters.

Rubella ("German measles") lasted longer than "three-day" measles but was a benign disease. It caused a red, bumpy rash, swollen lymph nodes around the ears and neck, and a mild fever. While the disease itself was relatively mild, German measles could cause severe birth defects if a woman became ill with it during the first months her pregnancy. However, mountain mothers did not know German measles caused birth defects until the late 1950s.

Today there is a vaccination that protects against measles, mumps, German measles, and chickenpox. This vaccine is given at age one and a half and again at ages four to five years. (9)

◆◆◆◆◆◆◆◆◆◆◆◆◆◆◆◆◆◆◆◆◆◆◆◆◆◆◆◆◆◆◆◆◆

Grandma Molly told us there were three kinds of measles–three-day measles, red German measles, and black measles. Three-day measles were just that–one day of fever followed by two days of a red rash and itching. Then they were gone.

German measles were a different story, according to Grandma. She warned of a high fever. Mom and Grandma forced hot liquids into us to make the measles pop out on our skin. "The fever is not gonna' go away until the measles pop out," she said. She made us get in the "living room" bed and she put dark blankets over the window to make the room dark. This was to protect our eyes. "Measles can make a kid go blind," Grandma Molly warned. "If the fever don't soon break, mix up some sheep manure tea and make them drink it."

When Grandma Molly recommended sheep manure tea, Mom rebelled against her treatment. "I ain't givin' my kids sheep shit tea," she told Aunt Goldie.

"I gave it to my kids," Aunt Goldie said. "Joyce was the last one to get the measles. They just wouldn't break out on her so I gathered me some sheep droppings and boiled it until the water turned brown. I strained it in a teacup and put in some sugar and about two ounces of moonshine. Joyce sipped a little bit of it, and I put her in the "living room" bed and wrapped her real warm. Before too long she was peppered with measles and sweatin' like a horse."

Some folks made pills out of sheep manure. They rolled the little balls in flour or powdered sugar. Sick children swallowed the little balls like pills. Others used sycamore bark tea and sassafras tea for measles. They would slice the outside part of the sycamore bark, leaving the gummy and slimy inside. This they boiled into a tea and served. Still another, more interesting method of bringing out the measles involved a horse collar. Immediately after removing the collar from a horse, the parent would push the child through the still-warm collar three times.

I have thought a lot about these cures for measles–the various teas, especially–and have concluded that it probably wasn't the content of the tea, but the hot liquid that brought out the measles. I suspect that Mom also knew that any hot liquid would serve the same purpose. She served us children hot lemonade when we had the measles.

Grandma Molly also warned us about black measles. "Black

measles are just that–the bumps on your skin are black," she said. "They turn you blind no matter if you cover the windows or not." When asked, Grandma could not cite any examples of people she knew who had suffered "black" measles. "I never knowed of anybody who got 'em. I just heard how bad they are," she explained.

Another one of Grandma Molly's medical gifts was the ability to "rub over" the mumps. One by one, we all came down with the mumps one summer immediately after school ended. One side of our jaws swelled first. Mom believed that if you had swelling from the mumps only on one side, then you could get them again. As each of us children came down with the mumps, she sent Dad to Hopkins Gap to ask Grandma Molly to "rub the mumps over." Grandma Molly would place her fingers on the swollen side and gently rub a line from that jaw, under your chin, and over to the opposite jaw. She would do it three times while saying the "words." The next day, both jaws would be swollen with mumps. She repeated what Mom had already told me, "You have to get them on both sides or you'll catch them again on the other side. Let's just get rid of them this time." By the time Grandma Molly died in 1971, children were being vaccinated and didn't need the mumps rubbed over anymore.

I never had such misery in my body as the mumps. You could get either "sweet" mumps or "sour" mumps, meaning that if you had "sweet" mumps and ate something sweet, the pain was almost unbearable. I guess I had "sweet" mumps, because all I wanted to eat was sour pickles.

Mom moved a bed into the living room, put me in it, and told me to stay there. We were supposed to stay in bed the whole time because, as we were told, the mumps could go "down on you" if you jumped or walked around too much. For girls, this meant the mumps would leave their jaws and settle in their ovaries. I never knew any girls who experienced this, but Mom's description of the pain led me to believe the victim never recovered enough to tell the full story. I remember that the pain from the mumps was such that I climbed out of the "living room" bed, slipped out the door, and went for long walks in the apple orchard. Remembering the warning that my mumps could go down on me, I walked very gingerly so I would not shake my aching jaws. My mumps stayed in my jaws in spite of my breaking the rules.

The mumps going down on boys was even more tragic. The disease left the jaws and moved into the testicles. "If this happens, they can't make babies when they grow up," Mom said. She told a story of one of her brothers who had the mumps to go down in one of his testicles. "All he had was girl babies, and he wanted a boy so bad. A boy has one testicle that makes girls and one that makes boys. It just depends on which one gets the mumps," she said.

Riding to the Doctor

Along with Grandma Molly's treatments, we also made occasional trips to Broadway to see Dr. Charles Watson. We had an old car that would not go very fast, and the graveled roads were bumpy like a washboard and filled with potholes. While it was only twenty miles from our house to Dr. Watson's office, the trip was long and rough.

The first time I remember seeing Dr. Watson was when I was four years old. I had an upset stomach with vomiting and diarrhea. I felt special because Mom and Dad were taking care of me, and I was able to sit on Mom's lap during the drive.

When we arrived at the doctor's office, Dad passed by it and then went up the street to turn around. He had to park the car on a downhill slope because it would not always start. When it did not start, he would put it into second gear and let it drift down the hill. When it reached a certain speed, he would let out on the clutch, and the motor would turn over enough to start the engine. I was always scared the car wouldn't start and we would be stuck in Broadway until God knew when. But the car always started with

Dad's tricking the motor with the clutch, and off we would go, chugging and bumping all the way back home.

On this trip to the doctor, Mrs. Watson, the doctor's wife came into the office while Dr. Watson checked on me. She had a banana in her hand, but the color was purple. She handed it to me and told me to eat it. I carried it in my hand all the way home. I never forgot that purple banana, although I don't remember eating it.

When we arrived home from the doctor, Mom opened the car door, took my left hand, and then lifted me out of the car onto the ground. She later told me, "When I sat you down on the ground I felt your arm slip out of your shoulder. You started screaming. I knew exactly what I'd done, so I picked you up and twisted your arm back into the socket." No wonder I don't remember eating the purple banana.

I asked Mom several times if she remembered the purple banana. She always said, "No, I never saw a purple banana. Your fever was so high; I think you dreamed about a purple banana after I put you in the "living room" bed and wrapped you up real warm." Dream or not, it was one of those events that made me feel very special. I wanted it to be true, and I still believe it was until this day.

Treatments of illnesses always reflect the times in which they occur. In isolated mountain communities, folks used what was available, and took advantage of the knowledge of the older women. The "living room" bed was an important part of the treatment, particularly where children were concerned. It took a long time for modern medicine to enter the mountains and replace the care handed out in the "living room" bed. In my lifetime, I experienced the transition from folk medicine to modern medicine. Even some of the "modern" medicine used fifty years ago now could be considered "ignorant" by modern-day medical standards.

Chapter 10

Practical Lessons about Work

"My father taught me to work. He didn't teach me to love it."
Abraham Lincoln

My generation of Appalachian Mountain children grew up in a time when most of our practical education still occurred at home, and our learning began soon after we left the "living room" bed to sleep in the loft. Each day, the grownups taught us new lessons that were meant to guide us into a future at least as successful as that of our older family members. We learned how to perform the necessary chores for survival, how to be a responsible and moral member of the community, and how to understand the portents of our immediate environment. We also learned how to avoid bad luck and to bring good luck, and how to read the signs given to us by our natural surroundings.

A Little Work Never Hurt Nobody . . .

Parents required their children to work around the house and the farm. Work often began as soon as a child could walk and before he or she left the "living room" bed. Often the mother gave the child a small basket to carry to the garden for vegetables or to take to the hen house as she gathered eggs. There were jobs for girls and jobs for boys and some jobs that crossed gender lines. Older boys and girls had to learn to milk a cow, feed the pigs, tend the chickens, and work in the vegetable garden. Girls' chores included washing clothes, cooking meals, making butter and cottage cheese, and taking care of the smaller children. Boys' chores included repairing fences and outbuildings, bringing in the crops such as corn, hay, and wheat, and killing the animals for the winter's meat. All these lessons were taught with an eye toward future roles as husbands and wives.

At very young ages, we knew what Mom had in mind for each day of the week. On certain days, I dreaded the upcoming chores, especially if it was hot summer time. The work started early every morning and I rebelled because the cool hours of morning were the best time for sleeping. We had no air conditioning and didn't know what it was. Air conditioning was opening the windows. The heat didn't stop Mom.

When we were children, Mom taught us a rhyme to let us know what the weekly work schedule was and what to do on each day. We didn't always follow the rhyme, but Mom liked to when we could.

Wash on Monday;
Iron on Tuesday;
Bake on Wednesday;
Clean on Thursday;
Churn on Friday;
Mend on Saturday;
Go to meetin' on Sunday.

The only time that Mom rescheduled her Monday washing was when the weather signs promised rain. After she made her fire in the kitchen stove on Monday morning, she would walk outside to check the smoke as it came out of the chimney. If it curled up into the sky, she proceeded with her plans to wash clothes and hang them out to dry. If the smoke curled toward the ground, she said, "We can't wash today. The smoke is coming down to the ground. It will be raining before I can get my clothes dry." I don't remember a time when she was wrong. To this day, I used this same sign to predict wet weather.

Rude Awakening

I was always relieved when Mom announced that the smoke was "coming down to the ground" because I dreaded Monday. On that day, Mom gathered up the dirty clothes and took the sheets off the beds. At least twice a year, she grabbed the curtains off the windows. "Get out of bed before the sun sours your guts," she'd call to us in her loud voice.

Often the sun wasn't up yet when she ran us out of bed, and I told her so. "The sun is not shining yet; how can it sour our guts?" I would ask.

"You heard me, get out of bed and bring your dirty sheets down with you so we can get the washin' started early," Mom would bark as she slammed the door with a loud bang at the bottom of the steps. After all that yelling and banging, the dead people in Gospel Hill Cemetery two miles away were turning over in their graves; all of us children were definitely awake.

I would punch Brenda in the back until she rose and helped me roll back the top cover and pull the sheets off the bed. That was not easy because when Mom made the bed, she had some method of tucking the sheets in at the bottom corners that made it seem they were sewn together. I always said a few dirty words that Brenda repeated to Mom as soon as her little feet reached the kitchen. I denied everything, stating that it was her word against mine. I knew all the time that Mom was too busy on Monday to go out in the yard and get a switch to whip my ass.

I asked Mom one time, "Why don't we just sleep on these sheets one more week?"

Her answer was, "They stink now. What do you think they

would smell like if we slept on them another week?" She was probably right since we didn't have a bath every day.

Doing the "wash" was a heavy and tiresome task. When I was very small, I was quite curious about how we washed the "wash." After I learned about nouns and verbs in school, I realized wash could be both a noun and a verb when Mom talked about "wash day."

Mom carried many buckets of water from the cistern in the back yard. Her buckets held three gallons of water each, and she carried two buckets at a time. After pumping them full, she carried them across the yard and up seventeen very steep steps through the back door and into the kitchen. There she kept the wringer washer in the corner between the table and wood stove.

I never forgot how many steps my mother had to climb to reach the kitchen because I once ran my tricycle down those steps. I believe my head hit on every step, and I counted as it banged into each one. There may have been more than seventeen steps, but I know my head hit seventeen times that day. However, that is another story.

After she reached the kitchen, Mom would lift the buckets up as high as her shoulders and pour the water into a large tub that she had set on the wood stove. She put wood in the stove and heated the water for the washing machine.

Mom had two zinc rinsing tubs that set on a platform right up against the washing machine. She had to fill both of those tubs with cold water from the cistern. While she waited for the water in the tub on the stove to heat, she poured Clorox into the washing machine, and added a little water to calm the fumes. She reached up on a shelf over the washing machine and grabbed a large cake of lye soap she had made the previous spring. Mom held the lye soap in her left hand, and with a peeling knife, she shaved off some slivers into the washing machine.

Lye Soap Making . . .

When I was about twelve years old, I watched my mother and grandmother make lye soap. Mom had been saving wood ashes throughout the winter and she explained to me that she was going to make soap with them. She saved the wood ashes from the kitchen stove in a homemade hopper. In Mom's case, it was a small wooden keg with a heavy wire mesh across the bottom. The bottom was lined with about six inches of straw. Periodically, she removed the ashes from the kitchen stove and poured them into the hopper on top of the straw. She explained to me that the straw kept the ashes from falling through the bottom of the keg when she started the soap making process.

The hopper set on top of a flat rock selected because it had a groove in it. When it was time to make soap, Mom poured a bucket of water on top of the ashes. The brown liquid that oozed through the straw came out the bottom of the hopper and followed the groove in the rock. It dripped into a small container placed at the edge of the rock. The brown liquid was the lye necessary for the soap-making process.

The next step was to fetch Grandma Molly to help with the soap making. Dad rose very early one spring morning and drove to Hopkins Gap to pick up Grandma Molly before he left home for work. The long day's work started immediately after breakfast.

This picture of a kettle filled with rendering pig fat demonstrates the kettle sitting on a kettle ring with the strategically placed tin pieces used to contain the fire.

Together, Grandma Molly and Mom set up an iron kettle in the back yard. It was set on a kettle ring that held it off the ground. Grandma Molly built a fire under the kettle and placed large pieces of tin around the sides of the kettle to contain the fire and hold the heat directly under the kettle.

Meanwhile, Mom went into the cellar and brought out a metal canister used to store lard from the previous fall butchering. She dipped the lard into the kettle and let it melt into liquid. When the lard had melted and was hot to the point of boiling, she and Grandma Molly added the lye to the mix.

Mom needed Grandma Molly to determine the amount of lard and lye to put into the kettle and to determine when the soap was done. Grandma Molly kept the amounts in her head and unfortunately, she never wrote them down; they went to the grave with her. After she died, Mom made her soap with store-bought Red Devil lye, which had a recipe for soap making on the container.

Mom and Grandma Molly stirred the mixture of lard and lye until soap emerged. I don't remember what type of stirrer they used, but others have explained that the best soap was made by using a paddle made from a sassafras tree. The stirring process seemed to me to go on forever; Grandma Molly and Mom took turns stirring for most of the day. When the mixture boiled up into a thick, foamy mass, the soap was done. When the mixture boiled, Grandma Molly stuck her finger in the soap and placed some on her tongue. At the time, I had no idea what she tasted it for, but after a few tastings and more stirring, she would say that the soap was done. Later on, Aunt Ethel told me that the soap was finished when a little dab on the tongue did not "burn" from the lye.

Grandma Molly asked Mom if she wanted "soft" soap or "hard" soap. At least at the time I was watching the process, Mom wanted hard soap. Grandma Molly told her to bring the saltbox from the kitchen. She poured out a handful of salt, sprinkled it over the foamy mixture, and stirred it once more. The salt acted to make the soap hard or soft–the greater the amount of salt the harder the soap.

Afterwards, my mother would douse the fire under the kettle with water and sweep off the pieces of tin used to contain the fire. She placed these over the top of the kettle so that the mixture in the kettle would cool, harden, and become soap over night. The next day, Mom took a long butchering knife and cut the soap out of the kettle. She cut it into cakes about four inches long and two inches thick. She placed it in two boxes, one for Grandma Molly and one for herself and the family. She placed our box on a shelf behind the washing machine. We delivered Grandma's soap the following Sunday.

◆◆◆◆◆◆◆◆◆◆◆◆◆◆◆◆◆◆◆◆◆◆◆◆◆◆◆◆◆◆◆◆

When the wash water was hot to the point of boiling, Mom used a small bucket to dip the water over into the washing machine. I loved the smell of the steam that wafted up out of the washing machine as the hot water mixed with the diluted Clorox and lye soap. The slivers of soap rapidly turned into fluffy bubbles of soapsuds. I enjoyed dipping my fingers into the hot soapsuds. The lye soap made the water soft and slippery on my hands.

Mom immediately put the "white" clothes into the steaming wash water. "My clothes smell better and are whiter than anybody else's," she often said. Mom was very critical of how other women did their wash. She constantly pointed out other women's "wash" hanging on the line and compared "level of whiteness" of her "wash" with women in Hopkins Gap and even women she didn't know.

When Dad drove us somewhere on Saturdays, she noted that some women had their "wash" hanging on the clothesline. "Look at that. I'll bet that wash has been hangin' there for days. No wonder it looks gray. Look how she hung things up with no rhyme or reason. She's got her white clothes mixed in with the coloreds. I could teach her a thing or two about washin'," she would say.

Once the white clothes were in the hot, soapy water, Mom

pulled a lever to start the dasher. It swished the clothes back and forth for an unspecified amount of time that Mom kept in her head. When she thought the clothes were clean, she stopped the dasher. She engaged the gears that turned the wringer, which consisted of two rubber rolls at the top of the washing machine. The rolls squeezed tightly together and rolled in opposite directions. They separated just enough to allow a piece of clothing to go through them.

Mom carefully lifted each piece of white clothing or sheet and shaped it into a thin piece that would go through the rubber rolls and fall into the clean, cold water in the first rinsing tub. The steam billowed up as the hot piece of clothing hit the ice-cold water.

Mom's hands would turn bright red from the hot water. Later in the day, she complained that the lye in the soap had "eat" at her hands until they were sore. She would show me the red cracks on her knuckles. When I was a little older, I silently wished that I could hire someone to wash for her or afford to take the clothes to the laundry.

My job was to separate the clothing as it came out of the wringer so that the clean water would remove most of the soap. When all the clothes were out of the washer and in the first tub of rinse water, Mom turned the wringer around so that she could wring out the clothes once more and let them drop into the second tub of rinse water. She reached up on the shelf and got a box of bluing for the final rinse water. She sprinkled the bluing in the water and stirred it with her hand.

"Most women I know use just one rinse water. I like to use two rinses to get all the soap out and put some bluing in to whiten my white clothes," she explained to me. "I believe that is why my clothes are whiter than anybody else's. Most women I know don't go to any extra trouble to get a white wash."

Using her hand, Mom would swish the clothes around in the second rinse water. She moved the wringer so that she could squeeze out the excess water for the last time. She set her clothesbasket on the floor under the wringer. The clean and twice-rinsed clothes fell into the basket and were ready to take outside to hang on the clothesline.

Mom kept a small tub with a batch of starch mixed in it next to the final rinse tub. She made her own starch by mixing a cup of flour with cold water. She then boiled additional water and poured the cold mixture in the boiling water. She let it cool and sieved it for lumps. When the clothing we wore came out of the wringer, she dropped them into the starch. After pushing them up and down in the starch, she ran them back through the wringer to remove the excess liquid.

Mom had a certain way that she hung the clean clothes on the clothesline. She hung all pieces of the same length side by side. First, she hung the sheets, then the bath towels, followed by dishtowels. After watching and helping her, I realized that she had taken the clothes out of the final rinse water in the same order that she was going to hang them.

"Mom, you are so smart and efficient," I told her in later years.

"It saves me digging around in the basket for the piece I want to put up next. It saves time," she explained. It was a small thing, but added to all the other efficient ways Mom had figured out to simplify her job as housekeeper, it made me respect her even more.

You're Wearin' and Eatin' Your Allowance

I don't know of any of my cousins from Hopkins Gap who received allowances to spend on themselves. I know that I never received an allowance. When I went to school outside Hopkins Gap, I learned from my classmates that some of them received small allowances each week. They used their allowances to buy ice cream after lunch at a little store in the school basement. I was jealous of the little bit of cash they flung around to show off. I asked Mom if I could get an allowance every week. She pointed to the food on the table and said, "There's your allowance and if that's not enough check out the clothes on your back. If you need more allowance than that, go find a job."

I thought that was hateful, since she wouldn't let me help Lloyd and Fannie Jane Myers shock wheat after I was twelve years old and started my period. She said it wasn't good for a young girl to be around a bunch of men; and, if I was having my period, the horses would go wild. Again, I thought all of that was just her excuse to keep me home to slave for her.

◆◆◆◆◆◆◆◆◆◆◆◆◆◆◆◆◆◆◆◆◆◆◆◆◆◆◆◆◆◆◆◆◆

Houseflies . . .

If I had to point to one chore that most mountain mothers had to do all the time, it was dealing with houseflies. Flies aggravated my mother more than all of her kids and our daddy put together. Flies were in every room in the house but nowhere did they swarm like they did in the kitchen. They crawled on the cabinets. They crawled on the stove. They crawled on the floor, the ceiling, and the walls. They swarmed the slop bucket on the back porch; and if you tried to sit on the front porch in the cool evenings, they crawled on your arms and legs. When Mom was older, flies bothered her so much that she offered her grandchildren a penny for each fly that they killed. Killing flies was the only job for which Mom offered compensation.

Mothers worried about houseflies getting on food that they were processing or about to put on the table for their family to eat. They used a variety of methods to get rid of flies. One method was to have a fly swatter available within easy reach. I remember Mom sitting on her little rocking chair, by the kitchen stove, while her supper was cooking. She kept her fly swatter nearby. She whacked every fly that came near her.

The mess that the flies left when Mom whacked them

really bothered her; therefore, she would not swat them on top of her cabinets where she prepared food. She waited until they landed on the front of the cabinet doors, the front of the stove, the walls, floors, and ceiling as far as she could reach. When one of us children walked into the kitchen, she handed the fly swatter to us. "Here, chase that fly off the cabinet. When it lands somewhere else, kill it for me," she said. We took the swatter and killed one or two more. We always scraped the dead flies off into the floor until the linoleum looked like the "killing fields."

After Mom had rested a while, she stood up, found her broom, and swept the dead flies into a pile. "Look, that's how many you can kill in a few minutes if you keep at it," she would brag. "Well I'll be damned," she would say, as she saw one or two of the seemingly crushed flies begin to wiggle back to life. "What do I have to do to get rid of 'em," she would mumble as she swept the pile into her dustpan, raised the lid on the wood stove, and dumped them in to burn. Another strategy that Mom used so that her entire day was not spent killing flies was to hire one of her grandchildren to kill them for her. Amanda, my sister's youngest daughter, was always hanging around Mom, watching her cook, and wash dishes. She told me, "I just loved to sit up on the sink and watch Grandma working in her kitchen."

One hot summer day the flies were buzzing around as usual, and Mom said to Amanda, "If you'll swat some flies for me, I'll pay you a penny for each one you kill."

Amanda said, "I got the fly swatter and went to work. I killed flies until I had to go home. Grandma never counted the number of flies I killed. I just kept a count in my head and told her how many when it was time to go. She always paid me. I never cheated her.

"One day I got the idea in my head that she probably didn't like crickets either. I had been seeing them on the back porch. I started killing them. When it was time to go home,

I told her I was charging her a nickel for each cricket I had killed. I said, 'Well, I killed fifty flies and that'll be fifty cents, and I killed five crickets. That'll be another quarter.' Grandma whirled around and looked at me. She said, 'I didn't tell you to kill no crickets, Amanda. When you kill a cricket, the cows give bloody milk. I ain't payin' you, and don't you kill any more crickets.' I promised her I wouldn't kill any more crickets."

Mothers also bought the flypaper that came in a small cardboard tube. You tacked it into the ceiling in each room and then pulled on the tube to unroll a piece of paper about two inches wide. The paper was almost dripping with a horrible sticky substance. The idea was that the flypaper would attract flies. When they would get their legs caught in the sticky stuff, they would die while trying to escape.

Flypapers were fine and dandy in theory; however, they had numerous disadvantages. First of all, tall visitors would walk into the house not noticing the flypaper hanging from the ceiling and bump their head into it. The flypaper, usually covered with dead flies, pulled loose from the ceiling. It ended up wrapped around their head and stuck in their hair. As they tried to remove it, sticky stuff covered their hands. The cursing that went on when that happened would burn these pages; thus, I won't repeat it.

Another problem with flypapers was that they were expensive. Those folks who made the flypapers took advantage of the poor housewives who wanted to serve clean food to their families. As I recall, they sold for about fifty cents for four. They didn't last very long because, at our house, we had so many flies that the fly paper filled up until there was no more room even for just one more fly to get stuck.

Mom could have used four flypapers a day adding up to fifty cents a day, or fifteen dollars a month, and one hundred and eighty dollars a year and that was just for one room–the kitchen. Hence, a good portion of the family income could have been spent on flypaper.

Another thing about flypaper that drove Mom crazy was that when the flies accidentally got caught, they did not leave this world without a lot of struggle. Each one tried to wiggle free of the sticky stuff and while wiggling, they buzzed and buzzed until the room was filled with a cacophony of dying flies stopping and starting their buzzing at various tones and pitches of their death throes. While we all enjoyed listening to them die, the sounds were irritating to say the least.

Perhaps the greatest disadvantage of flypapers was the fact that Mom stuck them in the ceiling close to the ceiling light string. This worked fine for her as she could find the string on the darkest night with little effort. However, the family member with the least practice in pulling the kitchen light string inevitably grabbed the sticky fly paper or bumped the string just enough to get it entangled in the sticky goo. It was both funny and tragic. I will let you imagine what happened.

During the times that mothers couldn't afford flypapers, they used other ingenious strategies to control the flies. My Mom used one that I rather enjoyed. It reminded me of a western cattle drive. She would round up us older children and arm us with towels. She would prop the kitchen door wide open. We started at the front of the house and waved our towels in the air to drive the flies toward the back door. We drove the flies through the living room, through the dining room, and finally out through the kitchen toward the open door. Mom always used her apron to bring up the rear. She untied the strings in the back and picked up the bottom. She waved it in the air to pull stray flies into the moving herd.

All the way through the house, she cursed the flies, "Get the hell out of my house. You've been out there crawling on fresh cow shit and hog shit and then coming in here to set on my cabinets and my food. I would like to stomp and pinch yer damned heads off one by one."

As the bulk of the flies went out the open door, Mom turned around with a smug look on her face. She closed the door behind the flies and tied her apron behind her back. She said, "Maybe I'll have some peace for a few minutes."

The "fly drive" did work quite well to chase the flies out the door; but they didn't go far. They just sat on the outside of the house and waited until the younger children went out to play. As soon as the door cracked open, ten or twenty zipped back into the kitchen. I wish I had a nickel for every time Mom yelled, "Stop runnin' in and out of the house. You're letting in flies. Don't hold that door open, damn it. I just chased the flies out."

Everybody had flies in their houses and as time passed many households invested in a fly sprayer. It was called the Flit spray gun. It was a tin can with a bicycle tire pump attached to it. Mothers filled the can with Flit, which was something like kerosene with a hefty portion of DDT, pointed the spout at the flying insects, or just around the room in general, and pumped.

In the early days of Flit, the flies plunged to the floor as dead as doornails when it hit them. As time went by, the flies seemed to be less affected by Flit. This could have been the time when the amount of DDT was being reduced because of its deleterious effects or maybe the flies were building up a resistance to Flit. I don't know.

What I do know is that every nook and cranny in the houses smelled like Flit for a long time after it was used. Everybody I knew smelled like Flit, and I am sure I smelled like Flit. A greasy film of Flit covered the furniture, stove, cabinet tops, and other places where food was laid for preparation.

Aunt Goldie bought a fly sprayer and loaned it to Mom. When the sprayer was just lying around our house, we picked it up and carried out spray battles with individual flies. Sometimes that was more fun than corncob battles with the Brown children who lived up the road.

Often when Mom placed the food on the table, she covered it with a sheet, pulled out the Flit sprayer, and doused the dining room so we could eat our food in peace with no flies buzzing our bread as we held it in our Flit-covered hands. Spraying the dining room was a mark of respect when company was sharing the meal.

In spite of the presence of the filthy flies crawling all over our food and the poisons used to try to control them, children rarely got sick with vomiting or diarrhea. The Flit spray did cause headaches; but they went away in a short while. I suppose children ate so much shit that got in their food off the flies' feet that they adapted to all kinds of bacteria and enjoyed life in spite of it. The DDT, however, is probably still in their bones awaiting an opportunity to rear its ugly head.

◆◆◆◆◆◆◆◆◆◆◆◆◆◆◆◆◆◆◆◆◆◆◆◆◆◆◆◆◆◆◆◆◆

Dish Washer, Hog Slopper, Corn Shocker

Being somewhat inventive, I did try to make some money throughout my childhood. For example, when I was about eleven years old, I washed dishes for Aunt Goldie, who had a factory job. She paid me twenty-five cents a week.

Aunt Goldie also asked me to feed a pig for her. I agreed to feed the pig twice a day until time to butcher. Aunt Goldie gave her son, Randy, money each week to buy a sack of hog feed, so I would have something to feed the pig. Instead of buying hog feed, he bought a cheap version of something called "feed dust." He kept the leftover money for himself. I tried to mix the feed dust with water when I went to feed the pig, but the dust just stayed on top of the water. I had to put my hands in the slop bucket so a little of the feed dust would mix with the water.

I never told Aunt Goldie what Randy was doing because he asked me not to tell her. He told me, "I buy Tarzan comic books with the extra money, and you know how much you like to read about Tarzan." That was a very true statement.

Tarzan comics came out once a month. Randy always bought one. When he finished with it, he threw it in the back seat of his car. I knew exactly which Sunday morning to check his back seat for the new comic book. My desire to continue reading Tarzan comics over came my sense of responsibility toward the poor little pig.

Even so, I faithfully fed the pig every day. When butchering time rolled around, Aunt Goldie concluded that the pig was not big enough to kill. I continued to feed the pig for nearly two years, and it never grew very much.

"Are you sure you are feeding my pig?" Aunt Goldie finally asked me.

"Yep, every morning and evening," I answered. Eventually, she concluded that there was something wrong with the pig, and sold it.

Aunt Goldie had never paid me for feeding the pig, so when she got her check from selling it, she came to my bed in the sleeping loft one Sunday morning and gave me a five-dollar bill. I had never held such a big bill in my hands. I was so proud at the time that I didn't calculate how much I had earned per day for feeding her pig for such a long time. Now I know my labor was cheap for Aunt Goldie. She made out okay from our financial relationships. She died a fairly wealthy woman.

When I was older, I tried to calculate how much I earned. However, when I divided three hundred and sixty five days times two and times two feedings per day into five dollars, the number I received was so small that I just shrugged my shoulders and tried to forget it. I had washed Aunt Goldie's dishes twice a day for five days and was paid a quarter a week. Twenty-five cents divided by ten is two and a half cents per dishwashing.

After both mathematical exercises, I simply concluded that I was a sucker, blinded by the five-dollar bill and the little shiny quarter. This should have taught me to draw up contracts with people for whom I was going to work. I also should have calculated the effort required relative to the income that I was to receive. Unfortunately, I still had a few more lessons ahead of me before I learned to negotiate a contract prior to the work I was about to do.

One of these lessons included my brothers, Larry and John. We were looking for work and we asked a farmer if we could shock his corn. The field was large. He wasn't sure we could do the work, but he let us try. We worked three days until all the corn was shocked into beautiful rows. All the time we were working, my brothers kept asking me how much we were going to earn. I assured them we would take home at least three dollars each. Once again, I had not negotiated a contract with the farmer.

When the work was done, he bragged about how nice his corn shocks looked. Then he reached into his pocket and handed each of us a quarter. My brothers were furious with me and the farmer. Larry wished the farmer some very bad luck and never forgot how humiliated we felt that day as we stood among the beautiful shocks of corn with a whole quarter in each of our hands.

Winter Time Income

It snowed deep and often when I was growing up. When the wind blew, the snow piled into deep drifts just on the other side of whatever the first barrier was that it blew up against. On one occasion, we had fifteen-foot drifts in the road past Aunt Goldie's house. The blowing snow hit the fence and fell onto the road. No vehicle could pass through the drifts. The regular snow scrapers tried to push the snow, but had no luck. Finally, after a week and a half with no school, a huge snow blower came through the road and made a path wide enough for the school bus to pass through. If it met a car, the bus or the car had to back up to find a place wide enough to pass.

Those days off from school afforded my brothers and me the opportunity to try our hand at making money by trapping muskrats. My cousin, Randy, had some steel traps that he let us use. We trudged through the snow over to Aunt Goldie's house, picked up the traps, and headed down the hill for Muddy Creek.

Sometimes the snow was as high as our knees, but we ploughed on through it. I remember thinking that if Mom asked us to bring in wood for the kitchen stove in the deep snow; we would complain and whine that it was too hard to walk. She often reminded us of our complaints about helping her when we returned from setting our muskrat traps. We explained to her that we were trying to make some money, because if we caught some muskrats, the skins were bringing a dollar and fifty cents each at Joe Kimble's junkyard.

Her response was, "Yeah, that money won't do me no good. You'll blow it all on candy and pop at Ress Kirkpatrick's store as soon as you get it." I knew she was right and didn't pursue the argument. There was something about having a little earned money in my pocket; it immediately started to burn a hole as I thought of the things I wanted to buy with it. It never lasted long.

◆◆◆◆◆◆◆◆◆◆◆◆◆◆◆◆◆◆◆◆◆◆◆◆◆◆◆◆◆◆◆◆◆

Ress Kirkpatrick's Store . . .

Ress Kirkpatrick lived up the road from Uncle Shirley's house. She made extra money by opening a tiny little store in one of her outbuildings. She sold basic groceries, such as canned food and packaged items, and she always kept a good supply of candy. When Dad and Mom took us to Uncle Shirley's for Sunday dinner, we carried our tiny earnings with us.

After dinner, we went into Uncle Shirley's "junk yard" where he collected old cars to mash up and haul to Pennsylvania to trade for a truckload of coal. He brought the coal back and sold it to families in Hopkins Gap, including my Mom. When he brought in a new bunch of old cars, my cousins, Billy Jean, Betty, and Nuck (Uncle Shirley's older children) invited us to play in the cars. We pretended we were driving; and then we discovered that we could find money if we turned over the seats and rooted around under the carpets in the car. We added whatever small change we found to the tiny earnings we had from the previous week, and up the road we went to Ress Kirkpatrick's store. We spent every penny on licorice, jawbreakers, bubble gum, and Tootsie rolls. We especially desired the bubble gum because each pack had a baseball card in it. My favorite card was Satchel Page. I wish I had those baseball cards today.

We ate all the candy on the slow walk back to Uncle Shirley's house; otherwise we would have had to share it with the smaller children. My dad despised chewing gum, so we stashed it to chew in the days to come when he wasn't around. This became very important after he popped a big bubble across my face once when he caught me blowing bubbles with my gum.

◆◆◆◆◆◆◆◆◆◆◆◆◆◆◆◆◆◆◆◆◆◆◆◆◆◆◆◆◆◆◆◆◆

When Larry and I arrived at Muddy Creek, we looked for muskrat tracks and slides. Muskrats dug holes back under the banks of the creek so that the water filled the hole up to about three quarters full, leaving an air space for them to come up out of the water and breathe. The muskrats occasionally came up on the creek bank, so there would be tracks and a wet and slippery mudslide where they slid back into their holes.

The steel traps had very strong springs in them. One end of the trap had a place where you could put your foot to open the mouth. One of us had to stand on the trap while the other one cocked the mouth open with a metal trigger. This was a dangerous activity for the one who had her fingers inside the jaws of the trap. It was important to have a good relationship with the person who had his foot on the trap to push the jaws open. Once we had the trigger set, we cautiously carried the trap to the creek. I must say we were good at what we were doing because not a single finger was lost in the process of setting our traps.

Occasionally, we would jiggle the trap too much as we carried it, and the trigger would work loose. The jaws snapped shut with merciless strength, making a loud noise that put the fear of God in anyone who had heard it. Hence, the caution we used in setting the traps. It was not hard to imagine the blood, tears, and misery of losing a finger or two in those jaws.

We gently set the traps just below the muskrat slides, placing them under water so that when the muskrat came out of his hole to go up the slide, he would unsuspectingly step on the trigger and catch his leg. Each trap had a long chain on it. Once the trap was set, we pulled the chain out into the grass and staked it into the ground. That prevented the muskrats from running off with our traps after they were caught.

We knew that most muskrat activity occurred before dawn, so we needed to check our traps as close to sunrise as possible. Muskrats had the nasty habit of chewing off their feet if they were caught in a trap, and it didn't take them long to do it. Our cousin, Randy, warned us that we probably didn't have much time to waste after the muskrat got caught in the trap. We learned the hard way that he was telling us the truth.

Because we didn't have school, we frequently did not get up early enough. We often found just a foot in our traps when we went to check them after breakfast. Sometimes the traps were thrown with no muskrat and no foot either. This meant that somebody else had gotten up earlier than we did and visited our traps. Our muskrat hide business ended with a fortune of about $3.00. From this experience, I learned that "the early bird gets the worm," or the muskrat, in this case.

Appalachian Mountain children worked hard from very young ages. We had no choice. Much of the work we had to do was not pleasant, and we were not expected to like it, just to do it. We cleaned manure out of stables, weeded the garden, carried wood into the house, and answered the beck and call of our parents and any other adult who needed our help. The question of compensation for our work was moot.

PART III:

ESTABLISHING A "LIVING ROOM" BED

Childhood for Appalachian children ended earlier in life compared to modern times. Most children in the generations before mine attended school until the seventh grade and finished at age fourteen. Teenage years and typical teenage behavior, as we know it today, did not exist. After finishing school, most children entered the next phase of the family life cycle–getting married, "going housekeeping," and starting a family of their own. Most young women married at very young ages–fourteen to sixteen years old. When young men finished school, they turned their attention toward earning money. They married when they were between the ages of eighteen and twenty-two.

It was very difficult to establish a household because poverty prevailed in the mountains. Most of the population owned no land of their own. Therefore, most young men became day laborers for nearby landed farmers, and others became migrant workers in that they moved from place to place as they followed seasonal work.

◆◆◆◆◆◆◆◆◆◆◆◆◆◆◆◆◆◆◆◆◆◆◆◆◆◆◆◆◆◆◆◆◆

No Land to Own in Appalachia . . .

In the Appalachian counties of Kentucky, Tennessee, Virginia, and West Virginia, less than two-fifths of the households owned land. In fact, the poorer half of the region's white settlers owned less than one percent of the land. By 1784, the vast majority of Southern Appalachia's lands had been redistributed to speculators and settlers through grants, military bounties, and public lotteries. Federal public land policies came too late to benefit Appalachia's poorer landless emigrants because this region had never come under the federal land system. As a result, Appalachian land was heavily concentrated in the hands of absentee owners and the region's wealthier settlers. By 1800, absentee landholders owned three-quarters of the total acreage reported in county tax lists. Consequently, there was little prospect for a poor young man to acquire land in Appalachia. (10)

◆◆◆◆◆◆◆◆◆◆◆◆◆◆◆◆◆◆◆◆◆◆◆◆◆◆◆◆◆◆◆◆◆

In Hopkins Gap, where my parents grew up, most of the land belonged to a small minority of early settlers or Shenandoah Valley farmers who did not live on their land. Young men had few options for making money from farming or timbering without the opportunity to own land of their own. Most became migrant workers for nearby land-owning farmers, logging companies, and fruit growers. My grandfather, John Wesley Morris, moved from job to job along with his wife and many children. My mother, the fourteenth child of eighteen children, was born in Twin Mountain, West Virginia, while her father was working in an orchard as a temporary job. Shortly after Mom's birth in 1920, the family moved back to Virginia to live just outside Hopkins Gap as tenant farmers. The final move, before my grandfather's death, was back to Hopkins Gap where he worked at many different temporary jobs.

Both Grandpa Morris and Grandpa Shifflett took odd jobs for local landowners. John I. Myers owned land on Feedstone Mountain. He cleared some of it and planted grass. He ranged his cattle there during the spring and summer months, and then he drove them back to the farm in the fall. Mr. Myers was friends with people in Hopkins Gap and he hired them to help with his seasonal farming. He hired both of my grandfathers–Austin Shifflett and John Wesley Morris–to help with spring planting and threshing. He also hired Garfield Crawford, Walter McDorman, and other men from Hopkins Gap to help with driving his cattle out of the mountains in the fall. Mr. Myers paid my grandfather's with checks.

On July 4, 1923, John Wesley Morris, my maternal grandfather, was paid $6.00 for several days of threshing for John I. Myers. Grandpa Morris signed the back of his check with his signature.

On October 13, 1927, Austin Shifflett, my paternal grandfather, was paid $35.00 for an unknown number of days of driving cattle from Feedstone Mountain to winter in Shenandoah Valley pastures. Grandpa Shifflett signed the back of his check with an X and a witness.

When my dad finished seventh grade at age fourteen, he worked for a large-scale moonshiner in Hopkins Gap. He received twenty-five cents a day for his labor. Most of my uncles on both sides of the family worked, at least part of their early lives, in that illegal profession. In fact, they had no choice other than to leave their home. These young men were not considered marriage material while they were earning money as moonshiners. Nearly every one of them spent time in prison for practicing their illegal occupation. When they met a girl and wanted to settle down and begin a family of their own, most engaged in legal day labor and moonshining became an avocation.

Establishing a household with a "living room" bed challenged young men and women in the mountains where the possibility of owning land slipped away before their time. Generations before them experienced the same situation; hence, a young couple saw their situation as normal and followed the traditions inherited from their forefathers and foremothers.

Chapter 11

Searching for a Mate

"The love game is never called off on account of darkness."
Thomas Masson

In the mountains of Appalachia, it was important to choose a proper mate to marry and then, to raise a family. A woman wanted to marry a man who would work hard and give her many children. He also needed to be a good daddy, both in kindness and in wealth. Unfortunately, many young people, including myself, observed that what one wishes for does not always happen. Some of my female cousins married men who did not provide well for their children. Over time, I suppose folks turned to magic to determine their future mates in an effort to avoid the terrible situations some of their relatives found themselves in after they spoke their wedding vows.

No one assumed that a child would want to remain single all of his or her life. All children were expected to marry and raise a family. I told Mom from the time I could put together enough words for a sentence that I would never marry. My declaration did not stop keep her from performing activities that may have affected my future marriage. For example, if I sat on a chair while she swept the floor, she made me move. She would never sweep around me. "Get up, Peg. I don't want to sweep around your feet. If I do, you will never get married," she said. I told her to go ahead and sweep around me; but she refused. Other beliefs about marriage included:

If you eat the last piece of food on a platter, you will be an old maid or bachelor.

If a person always sleeps alone, they will never marry.

Lift your feet when you ride over a creek, if you want to get married some day.

I based my early decision never to marry on my observations of how men treated women in the patriarchal Appalachian hills. The roles were clearly defined. Boys would grow up and get a job or a trade. Girls would grow up, marry one of the local boys, and start having children immediately. My own birth is a witness to that plan for women. I was born nine months and ten days after Mom and Dad's wedding.

Young Girls Search for a Mate with Magic

All young girls practiced magic to see if the men they were interested in were also interested in them. All around the calendar, they used whatever was available to see into the future. Sometimes a special day of the year and sometimes certain qualities of plants or fruit predicted the future mate. For example, the first day of May was a time of powerful prediction and associated with ancient fertility rites. Because these rituals were a part of the culture, I practiced them along with my female cousins and classmates.

May 1st . . .

Many cultures around the world recognized the first day of May as a special time. During the Middle Ages, May Day was a regular feast day in England and on the continent of Europe. People erected maypoles and young girls whirled around them in a fertility dance. This custom continued in America until some religious groups in New England banned it. However, in more remote rural areas, many schools celebrated May Day until the mid 1950's. At Mt. Clinton Elementary School, attended by Hopkins Gap children, we looked forward to May Day celebration. It was about boyfriends and girlfriends. One young girl was chosen as the "Queen of May." A May Pole was erected on the front lawn of the school. The pole had colorful ribbons fastened to the top of the pole.

A May Pole dance (Courtesy of the Library of Congress)

Loretta Coakley and the author, Peggy Shifflett pose for a picture at Mt. Clinton High School in their May Pole dancing clothes. (Picture Courtesy of Loretta Coakley.)

Female dancers wove in and out as they danced around the Maypole. The ribbons formed a colorful plait as they wrapped around the pole. The dancers then retraced their steps exactly in order to unwind the ribbons. Maypole dancing has its roots in Germanic pagan fertility symbolism.

In ancient times, folks believed that April 30th was one of four witches' Sabbaths. They built fires during the night to burn away the witches. April 30th had various names–in England it was Roodmas and in Germany, it was Walpurgis. Folks believed the air of May 1st morning was pure and May 1st morning dew had healing qualities because of the fires that had burned the night before. (11)

◆◆◆◆◆◆◆◆◆◆◆◆◆◆◆◆◆◆◆◆◆◆◆◆◆◆◆◆◆◆◆◆◆◆

Folks all along the Appalachian Mountains believed the air and the dew of May 1st was pure. Some folks used the dew that fell on May 1st to wash away their freckles. They arose before sunrise, dressed without talking to any person, walked downstairs backward, proceeded to a grassy spot wet with dew, rubbed their hands in the dew, and washed their face with the moisture. The person addressed the morning with:

Good morning to you, Mrs. May.
I've come to wash my freckles away.

Beyond pure air and healing dew, any rain that fell on May 1st had curative uses. For example:

Wash your hair in May water, and you will have good health all year.

Run bareheaded in the rain on May 1st and you will not have any headaches the rest of the year.

If you get wet on May 1st, you will not catch a cold or get sick for a year.

To cure sore eyes, take May water, place straws broken up fine in a vessel with the water, let the concoction stand, pour off the water, then place the damp straw material over the sore eyes.

More important, on May 1st, Appalachian Mountain girls learned something about their future spouses. We were told to:

Go out in the afternoon of the first day of May and pull two fresh, new poplar leaves. Lay them on the ground and place a snail between them. Go back the next morning, and you will find your sweetheart's name written, by the tracks of the snail, on the poplar leaves.

In the morning, on the first day of May, take a pan and place about one inch of cornmeal in the bottom, place two or three snails in the meal. The snails will crawl and form the first letter of your sweetheart's name.

When the sun is shining on the first day of May, hold a mirror over a pool of water and you will see the image of your sweetheart's face.

Take a handkerchief to an oat field the first night in May. Spread it out on the oats. The next morning early you will see the initials of the man you are going to marry written in dew on the handkerchief.

Christmas time offered possibilities for learning the name or initials of future spouses. For example, a bucket of water placed in the barnyard on Christmas Eve would freeze solid and bulge on top. In the morning, the lines in the ice displayed either the initials or entire name of the future mate. An aged woman from West Virginia told about her attempt to determine if she would have a future mate. She said, "On Christmas Eve, I went to an abandoned barn and held the end of a ball of twine in one hand and threw the ball with the other hand. The ball went into an opening in the building. I gradually started winding the twine back up around my hand and when the ball caught on something, I knew my future husband was on the other end."

During the spring and summer months, young women used certain plants to determine if they were loved by a real or imaginary boy. One was the dandelion, a plant that served several purposes for the region, which they used in prognosticating. The dandelion leaves were among the earliest arrivals each spring and provided one of the first means for fresh greens after a long winter without leafy vegetables. The plant was served as a salad, but the golden blossoms were also gathered and made into a wine that was considered a respectable and pleasurable beverage.

Young girls found another use for the dandelion when it was in seed. If she was able to blow all the seeds from the pod in three attempts, it meant she would have a successful and happy marriage. Some girls reported that the same practice meant the person would marry within the year.

The daisy was another plant oracle. The girl would pick a single blossom from a daisy plant. She plucked each petal from the blossom and said:

Rich man, poor man, beggar man, thief,
Doctor, lawyer, merchant, Indian chief.

The occupation named as she plucked the last petal foretold the status of the young girl's future spouse. Inquisitive young girls picked a second blossom, by which they sought to learn in advance the quality of home they would live in after marriage. As she plucked each petal from the daisy blossom, she said:

Big house, little house, pigsty, barn.

Finally, unusually curious girls used the daisy to foretell the kind of bridal gown they wear on their distant wedding day. As she plucked each petal from the daisy blossom, she said:

Silk, satin, calico, rags.

Apples had an unusually meaningful place among the mountain residents in earlier times, and little wonder. Folks ate the apple as a fruit, baked it into luscious pies, boiled it into apple butter, sliced and dried it into snits, pressed it into cider, and, at times, distilled it into brandy.

This fruit also foretold a person's future spouse. Young girls often used the seeds to determine if a special boy was interested in her. She named the apple for the boy, sliced it open, and removed the seeds. As she counted each seed, she said:

One, I love
Two, I love
Three, I love, I say,
Four, I love with all my heart,
And five, I cast away;
Six, he loves,
Seven, she loves,
Eight, they both love;
Nine, he comes,
Ten, he tarries,
Eleven, he courts,
Twelve, he marries.

If you break the top of a mullein stalk and it continues to grow, your sweetheart loves you. If it does not grow, your sweetheart hates you.

During summer, buzzards circled overhead above a dead animal or floated on a warm breeze. We recited a rhyme to the buzzard so that we could find out the direction of the house of our future sweetheart.

Turkey buzzard,
Fly to the east, and
Fly to the west, and
Fly to the one that
I love the best."

After saying the rhyme, we watched the buzzard fly away. If it flapped its wings three times before it flew out of sight, then the sweetheart you were thinking about loved you.

On Halloween night, a group of girls would spend the night with a girl who lived near a creek. At midnight, they would rise and walk backward to the stream. When they arrived, they would look backward over their left shoulders into the water, and they would see the face of their future husbands.

There were certain things to watch for on any holiday. These items had different meanings, such as the occupation of your future husband, what his nature would be, your luck in your future marriage, and whether you would marry into money. On a holiday, if you saw a:

Blackbird	*your husband would be a clergyman*
Cardinal	*your husband would be a sailor*
Crossbill	*your husband would be quarrelsome*
Dove	*you will have good luck in marriage*
Goldfinch	*you will marry a millionaire*

To induce a dream to reveal a future spouse, you could place your shoes in the shape of a "T" then say:

I place my shoes in the shape of a "T"
My future husband I dream to see.
Color of eyes, color of hair,
And the everyday clothes he will wear."

From very young ages, girls seemed obsessed with whom they would spend their adult lives. Boys, on the other hand, did not practice magical rituals to find a future mate.

In spite of the hardships of their parents and grandparents before them, young girls and boys continued to play the game of love until they found the one with whom they wanted to raise a family. Most of the time, the future mate lived in the same mountain community. Without online dating and matchmaking, girls turned to magic to determine who was to be the special young man for them.

Chapter 12

Courtship and Marriage

"Marriage is the agreement to let a family happen."
Betty Jane Wylie

Once a boyfriend or girlfriend appeared, the courtship was simple and short. Courting took place within the confines of work and community. Young people saw each other at school, at church, at apple butter boiling, hog butchering, corn husking, and other survival-related events. Specific rituals and signs allowed for courting during these events. For example, during a corn husking, the person who found a red corn ear had to kiss someone of the opposite sex that he or she found attractive. The kiss was an invitation to court, and it often was incentive enough. If a young boy or girl was interested in someone who was helping with the husking, the search for the red ear of corn speeded up the process of getting the job done.

During apple-butter boiling, courting couples stirred the kettle with both holding on to the stirring paddle. Each time the paddle bumped the sides of the kettle, they kissed. The kissing consequence of bumping the sides of the apple butter kettle encouraged couples who were attracted to each other to help with the stirring; hence, the job was easier for the older folks.

As time passed and movies were invented, courtship became

more modern. For example, my dad rode to Harrisonburg with his brother, and Mom rode with her sister, Goldie. They met Uncle Shirley (and his girlfriend at the time) at Layman's restaurant or the Daily Lunch for a hot dog. Then they went to a movie or a show. Mom told me, "We saw Gene Autry on stage in Harrisonburg. We saw a lot of movies too."

After the show, Mom and Dad returned with their ride to their respective homes, which were about three miles apart. During the week, they wrote letters to each other describing how much they loved and missed each other. In one letter, Mom asked Dad to marry her. He accepted her proposal in a letter dated June 21, 1940. They were married on July 27, 1940.

Women immediately started having children. Again, witness my own birthday, which came nine months and ten days after Mom and Dad's wedding day. Mom told me, "When people saw that I was pregnant, they started counting on their fingers back to the date of my marriage and tryin' to figure if I 'had to' get married. Even after your birth, a lot of people thought I was knocked up with you and that's why we got married."

Even though many young girls were pregnant when they got married, it was still considered a shame when it happened. My grandmother, Mary Lam Morris, was pregnant with her first child when my grandfather, John Morris, married her. He was twenty years old. She was fourteen years old. She gave birth to the first child prior to her fifteenth birthday.

Because of the isolation in the mountains, occasionally young people with the same last name would start courting. When this occurred, family members cautiously searched their background to determine if the boy and girl were closely related. If they found that the couple was closer than second cousins, the courtship was discouraged. First cousins were not allowed to court; but second cousins could court.

Often a brother and sister from one family would choose to court a brother and sister from another family. The offspring from these unions were called "double first cousins," and folks assumed they were closer to each other than regular first cousins. In Hopkins Gap, two of my female cousins with the last name Crawford married two brothers from another Crawford family. These unions made their children "double first cousins" with the same last names.

Another situation that occurred, at least where I grew up in the mountains, came about because young men sowed their wild oats among the young girls without benefit of marriage. The older members of the community kept track of who had fathered whom and passed it down as time went by. Occasionally, two people with the same father would become attracted to each other and begin to court. Soon, folks would gossip about so-and-so, and note that they were really half brother and sister because so-and-so had fathered both of them. Eventually the couple would learn of the problem and abruptly end the courtship.

Marriage

In earlier times in American society, both men and women had great social pressure on them to marry. Marriage was regarded as a social obligation and an economic necessity. Nearly all adults married. If a woman had not married by the age of twenty, it was socially humiliating to her family.

If an "older" daughter remained single, her only hope was to marry a man who lost his wife in childbirth and needed a woman to care for his young children, him, and his home. My step-grandmother, Ivy Lam, was a case in point. When Grandma Mary died after the birth of her eighteenth child, Grandpa John tried to care for his underage children himself for two years. Finally, he walked down the road to John Lam's house and asked for the hand of his twenty-two year old daughter. John Lam agreed and the wedding occurred shortly after.

Marriages were mostly for economic benefits, not romantic

situations. This fact determined how the weddings occurred. Rarely, if ever, did marriages occur in church. Most couples dressed up in their best clothing and went to the courthouse where they were married by a judge with just a witness or two in attendance. Since poverty prevailed, there were no honeymoons. Frequently, the couple would reside at the bride's home the first night, and sometimes reside in the home for six months to a year. The groom's ability to make enough money to rent or build a house determined the length of stay at the bride's home.

My Grandpa John Wesley Morris poses with his new bride, Ivy, (on the right) and his new sister-in-law, Sarah, on the left. (Circa 1929) (Picture courtesy of Debbie Pryor)

A wide variety of practices, beliefs, and sayings developed over time in association with marriage, probably because it is one of the most important social events in the life of an individual and in society. Much of the traditional lore collected along the Appalachian Mountains is similar to that found in American society in general. For example, folks recited the sayings "Happy is the bride that the sun shines on," and the rhyme stating what the bride should wear for her wedding: "Something old, something new, something borrowed, and something blue."

A few beliefs and practices seemed unique to the mountains. For instance, weddings started on the half-hour because of the belief that the hands of the clock should be moving upward during the ceremony to bring good luck to the marriage. Also, some folks placed an old penny into the bride's right shoe. As the bride took her first step away from the ceremony as a newly married woman, the right foot stepped first thus bringing good luck.

Mountain folks also believed the bride had to be careful about the color of the dress she wore at her wedding:

Married in white, you've chosen right.
Married in green, ashamed to be seen,
Married in gray, you will go far away.
Married in red, will wish you dead,
Married in blue, love ever true,
Married in yellow, ashamed of your fellow.
Married in black, you will wish yourself back.
Married in pink, of you only he will think.

We had rhymes about the season of the year that a person should marry:

Marry when the year is new—
Always loving, kind and true.
When February birds do mate
You may wed, nor dread the fate.
If you wed when March winds blow,
Joy and sorrow both you'll know.
Marry in April when you can,
Joy for maiden and for man.
Marry in the month of May
You will surely rue the day.
Marry when June roses blow,
Over land and sea you'll go.
Those who in July do wed
Must labor always for their bread.
Whoever wed in August be
Many a change are sure to see.
Marry in September's shrine,
Your living will be rich and fine.
If in October you will marry,
Love will come, but riches tarry.
If you wed in bleak November,

Only joy will come, remember.
When December's snows fall fast,
Marry and true love will last.

Of course, we had a rhyme about the day of the week that was best for marrying:

Wed on Monday, always poor
Wed on Tuesday, wed once more
Wed on Wednesday, happy match
Wed on Thursday, splendid catch
Wed on Friday, poorly mated
Wed on Saturday, should have waited
Wed on Sunday, Cupid's wooing;
Wed in the morning, quick undoing.

In my parents' generation, there were few if any formal church weddings; and, in fact, my parents were married in a group ceremony with three couples saying their vows at the same time. The three couples divided the cost of the minister to save money.

I asked Mom where she and Dad went for their honeymoon. She said, "We rode around all evening with Hattie and Earl. They got married with us. We just visited friends we knew." In other words, the new couple spent the evening of their wedding visiting in the community. They spent their wedding night at Uncle Rob and Aunt Goldie's house, which was where Mom lived.

◆◆◆◆◆◆◆◆◆◆◆◆◆◆◆◆◆◆◆◆◆◆◆◆◆◆◆◆◆◆◆◆◆

Wedding Night Shivaree . . .

When neighbors and friends found out where the bride and groom were spending their first night as a married couple, they paid a visit. Along with them, they brought pots and pans, shotguns, cowbells, and an occasional stick of dynamite. This was a *shivaree*–a wild wedding night serenade of violent noise and prank-playing. The noise continued until the newlywed couple came to the door and invited the group in for drinks and food. If the couple did not come out, the merry-makers crashed in the door and dragged the couple from their bed. The revelers placed the newlyweds on a horse. Someone fired a shotgun to scare the horse, and off the newlyweds galloped through the woods and fields. Whatever happened to the newlyweds, the *shivaree* was intended as a complimentary sign of approval of the new couple. (12)

◆◆◆◆◆◆◆◆◆◆◆◆◆◆◆◆◆◆◆◆◆◆◆◆◆◆◆◆◆◆◆◆◆

While the young couple stayed with the bride's parents, they gathered or made goods to set up a household. Meanwhile, the groom came and went, sometimes for meals, sometimes to stay overnight. The location of his work determined how much time he spent with his new wife. The couple "went housekeeping" after the groom earned enough money and found a house.

Mom stayed with Aunt Goldie and Uncle Rob for several months as Dad bought necessary household items from each paycheck. Finally, they rented a house on Muddy Creek from John I. Myers and started their first home together.

Thus, the rituals of courtship and marriage, under control of the community, confirmed family ties and led to a new economic and loving relationship between two people. To begin their family in the warmest place in their home, the young couple placed a "living room" bed close to the stove in the living room.

PART IV:

THE END OF LIFE

The "living room" bed served the family as children were born, when family members were ill, and finally, when the end of their lives drew near. Up and down the Appalachians, folks recognized the term "living room" bed and acknowledged it as a place for end of life rites.

"Yes, I know about the "living room" bed," one older woman immediately said when asked. "My mother died at home in our living room. We all stood by her side as she took her last breath."

Another woman told the story of her grandmother, who died at home in the "living room" bed. "My mother told me that after a person died in the "living room" bed, you could find a crown made of feathers in the pillow that the person's head was on. You won't believe me, but I was there when Momma cut the pillow open after Grandma died and showed me the crown," she said.

Stories abounded about the signs of coming death. Those included visions, dreams, sightings, strange animal behavior, and hearing strange noises. Neighbors, friends and families passed long hours together in a solemn ritual known as "sittin' up with the dead." During this time, they shared stories about the loved one who was dying as well as deaths that occurred in the past.

I first experienced death when I was five years old. My uncle, Earl Stoutemyer, dropped dead of a heart attack after a bird flew into our front window and died. In that same year, my Uncle

Rob died of complications of gallbladder surgery. Sadly, I learned during Uncle Rob's funeral that not all family members attended a funeral to offer condolences and assistance to the bereaved. It was a difficult lesson for someone so young.

In 1958, at age fourteen, my grandpa, Austin Shifflett, died at home in the "living room" bed. The hours of "sittin' up with the dead" and his funeral represented the typical traditional Appalachian Mountain treatment of death and burial. Grandma Molly carried out the rituals that people thought were necessary if a soul was to leave the house. In anticipation of my grandfather's death, she purchased a new black dress to wear before and after the funeral. She wore black clothing for a year after Grandpa Austin's death. Grandma Molly insisted that the funeral home return Grandpa Austin's body to their house prior to burial. His daughters and neighbors took turns "sittin' up with the dead." Friends and neighbors cooked and brought food for the family and those who came to offer their condolences.

Chapter 13

Death Along the Appalachians

"Let children walk with Nature, let them see the beautiful blending and communions of death and life, their joyous inseparable unity, as taught in woods and meadows, plains and mountains and streams of our blessed star, and they will learn that death is stingless indeed, and as beautiful as life."

John Muir

Because mountain people lived in isolated hollows with extended family members nearby, deaths occurred at home well into the 1950s. Extended family members, friends, and neighbors gathered around the dying person as he lay in the "living room" bed and took his last breaths. Therefore, at the end of life, the "living room" bed became a nursing bed and ultimately a deathbed.
Medical treatment for the ill and dying was available, but the ride was rough and the distance far. In the days of my parents' and grandparents' generation, from the 1880s through the 1950s, death was a common event. It was normal for a family to lose one-third of their offspring to stillbirth or "second summer sickness."

Throughout my childhood, Mom shared stories of babies and young children who had been lost from her family. For example, Mom was the fourteenth of eighteen children. Only twelve lived to adulthood. She often talked about a little girl sister named Vivian. She died when Mom was about three years old.

"I always heard that Vivian was as beautiful as an angel. Nobody was surprised when she died. They all believed she was an angel from God," Mom said.

She often spoke of Charles Payne, the son of Mom's sister, Stella and Clarence Payne. Charles died at age fourteen from rheumatic fever. She frequently described his suffering from pain in his legs as well as his death in the "living room" bed at his home. "I wasn't very old, but I remember Charles trying to get his breath just before he died," she said. "Everybody started crying and said that it wouldn't be long before he was dead because he had the death rattles." The death rattles were the sounds the dying person made in his or her throat as the lungs filled with fluid.

Families remembered the tragic deaths of their children by carving epitaphs into stone. A stroll through most any graveyard in the mountains revealed the sorrow of these events. When I visited a cemetery, I would stop for a moment and reflect on the tears that were shed on each spot as the family said goodbye to a little child. Epitaphs carved on tiny tombstones, which were sometimes topped with lambs, memorialized those tears:

Our sweet little man is at rest,
He is calling us all to come home
And be with him.

Five little angels to guard my bed,
One at the foot and one at the head,
One to sing and one to pray,
And one to carry my soul away.

This tender bud so young and fair
Called hence by early doom,
Has gone to show how sweet a flower
In Paradise may bloom.

Our little lamb is in the upper fold,
From heat of summer and from winters cold,
Safe from earth's troubles and its dreams untrue,
Our little lamb is waiting for you.

God needed one more angel child
Amidst his shining band,
And so he vent his loving smile,
And clasped our darling's hand.

It was common for a family to lose two small children at the same time, perhaps to German measles, pneumonia, or rheumatic fever.

Brother and sister gone for a time,
Wait for the others, coming sometime,
Safe with the angels whiter than snow,
Watching for dear ones waiting below.

Rites of Passage . . .

Anthropologist Arnold Van Gennep noted that life transitions in many cultures follow a recognizable pattern of behavior. He described rites of passage as special rituals societies use to assist their members at key times of change, such as puberty, marriage, and death. Rites of passage have three phases: separation, transition, and re-incorporation. Van Gennep constructed this scheme to describe patterns of life in those traditional societies or communities of relatively few people and high levels of face-to-face contact. The rites of passage surrounding death have two purposes: to assist the dead as they pass from the world of the living to the world of the dead; and to assist the living as they adjust to new statuses and roles in the absence of the deceased. The actual physical dying ***separates*** the deceased from their living statuses of father, brother, or husband, and mother, sister or wife.

The ***transition*** phase consists of preparing the dead for burial followed by behaviors symbolic of status changes for the living. This is a time of uncertainty and potential danger. Those still living consider the corpse impure because of its inability to respond to loved ones, yet it is still "present" in their everyday routine. In this phase, the deceased is neither what they were but not yet what they will become. During transition, extended family and friends adjust to the death by paying their respects to the dead, noting their previous identity with them, and expressing sorrow for the bereaved to reaffirm their continuing relationship to them. Often-heard statements such as "If you need anything, anything at all, just let me know," express these sentiments. Those closest to the deceased display their changed statuses through symbols–the widow dons a black dress, for example. The deceased is extolled as a good person in thought and deed. This is a way of letting go of past transgressions and easing the transition of the deceased into the next world. Burial or cremation is the final aspect of the transition phase.

The ***Re-incorporation*** phase consists of the entire grieving community returning to the home of the deceased for a meal. This phase brings family and friends together as a group without the presence of the deceased. New statuses begin to emerge at this ritual meal. For example, those present shake the hands of the oldest son or daughter and welcome them as the new head of the family. (13)

◆ ◆

Portents of Death

Older generations who lived along the Appalachian Mountains held on to many beliefs about death, and they passed these on to my generation. Folks at the "living room" bedside of a dying person discussed the signs of the imminent death. Some said they heard a screech owl calling before dark or a dog barking at midnight during the days leading up to the death. Family members related stories of how the dying person said that he or she talked to dead family members one or two nights before his or her death.

My brother, Larry, died in 2006. He told his wife, Hilda, that Mom and our cousin, Ruby, came to his hospital room, and talked with him. Both had died several years before. Larry died within two days of telling this story. One woman told me that she woke in the night and saw a vision of her mother, dressed in a long white gown, standing at the foot of her bed. "The vision scared me, and I wondered why I would be scared of my mother," she said. "I never told anybody about what I saw. Two days later, Momma dropped dead of a massive heart attack."

In talking with people along the Appalachian Mountains, I heard that birds were very important in predicting a death. Birds pecking on a window, accidentally flying into the house, or flying against a window and dying were signs of an upcoming death. Special messages of death came from owls that screeched nearby or landed in the yard.

Dogs, cows, spiders, crows, worms, and roosters all had their usual ways of behaving, but a change in their behavior meant someone was going to die. When dogs howled after midnight or howled in front of a house at night, it was a sure sign of death. When cows mooed after dark or a crow sat on the roof of the house, a death would soon occur inside the house. If a rooster crowed after sundown, someone close by would die. If a spider wove a web in front of you, news of a death soon followed. If a person had a measuring worm walking on their clothing, it meant they were being measured for a shroud. A sure sign of a death in the family came with the crowing of a laying hen. Mom once killed a hen as soon as it started crowing like a rooster. We ate her for supper the very day she crowed.

Keeping a watchful eye toward events around the home

informed the family of an upcoming death. For example, if a picture fell from the wall, someone would die. A grandfather's clock which had not been running would strike when someone was about to die in the home in which it stood. If you carried a shovel or a pitchfork into the house, someone would die. This was a significant sign for Mom. She went crazy when we thoughtlessly brought a shovel or any garden tool into the house.

"You will be digging a grave with the shovel," she warned if we forgot and carried a garden tool into the house. If it was a pitchfork, she said, "You will be pitched into hell by the devil." When she saw us with our tools, she would yell, "You turn right around and get that out of here through the same door you brought it in." Mom believed you could change the bad luck if you took the tool out the way you brought it in.

Mom grew very upset if one of us children rocked a rocking chair with no one sitting in it. "Stop rocking that chair!" she yelled. "You will cause somebody to die." Even when we rose up out of a rocking chair, we learned to stop it from rocking before we walked away.

All along the mountains, I discovered folks who had heard about careless behaviors that could cause a death. For instance, it was bad to allow a baby to look into a mirror. A baby who saw its own image would die before it was a year old. I heard that a person should never start sewing a new item of clothing for a person on a Friday, or the person who was to wear it would die before it was finished.

As children, we learned that when one person in the community died, two more would follow within three months. When one of our relatives died, Mom would sadly announce, "You mark my words–there will be two more deaths before it's over."

Mom loved the willow trees that grew along muddy creek near Bob Showalter's house. She watched their long branches swing in the breezes as she shook her head. "I would love to have a willow tree, but when a willow tree is planted, the person who planted it will die when the tree is big enough to cover a grave. I thought about that when Fannie Jane [Myers] planted the willow tree near [her son,] Carroll's, house. Sure enough, it wasn't long before she died of cancer," she said.

News of a death in the community spread rapidly up and down the hollows. Preparations for the funeral began immediately, especially before embalming became available. Some folks remembered their grandmothers and aunts gathering around the dead body, cleaning it, and dressing it. They placed the body on a plank, laid the hands across the chest, closed the eyes, and put a penny on each eyelid to keep it shut. Folks often described the most evil person in a community by saying, "Why he's so mean, he would steal the pennies off a dead person's eyes."

One older woman remembered her grandmother putting a cloth under her dead grandfather's chin. She pulled his mouth shut and tied the cloth on top of his head until rigor mortis set in. "Grandma told me that would keep his mouth from hanging open," she said. After cleaning and dressing the body, family members placed it on display in the living room. Folks arrived with food for the family and the friends who helped with "sittin' up with the dead." They viewed the body on their way out the door.

One custom told to me by several people had to do with "telling the bees" that the master or mistress of the house was dead. This practice was not very common; however, it did occur in a few instances. Many homesteads had a special corner in a field where they kept a cluster of beehives. The owners gathered the honey to use as a sweetener; it was an important ingredient in many home remedies. Some folks believed that when the owner of the bees passed away, the bees swarmed and left the homestead. To keep this from happening, someone close to the deceased would venture to the beehives and cover each of them with a black cloth. After the hives were covered, the person recited a little verse:

"Stay at home, sweet bees
Don't fly away.
Master [or Mistress] _____ is dead and gone."

Sittin' Up with the Dead

Family members and friends, most always women, stayed with the body around the clock until the burial. People gave me several reasons for this part of the funeral ritual. Before embalming, family members wanted to make sure the person was truly dead. Therefore, they watched the corpse for signs of breathing and movement. Another reason was to keep the cats away from the body because of the belief that the cat could steal the soul of the dead person or actually eat parts of the body. Another reason was to keep the houseflies off the corpse, particularly in the summer months. While "sittin' up with the dead," the women told horror stories about people who were buried alive, a fact later discovered after their graves were opened for some reason.

My earliest memory of Mom talking about death happened when we still lived in the four-room storehouse with the cement-slab front porch. I was five years old. My dad had just returned from World War II. Mom stepped out on the back steps one night to empty her dishwater. She suddenly jumped back into the kitchen, slammed the door, and sat down on a chair. Her face was as pale as a sheet. Mom pulled me close to her and said, "I just saw something white coming around the end of the house."

"What was it?" I asked. I was scared; I am sure my little brain tried to imagine what would be outside in the dark.

Mom answered, "I think it was my momma's ghost and if it was, somebody in the family's gonna die."

"Our family?" I asked. I am sure I was wondering which one of us it might be. Mom looked at me and realized she had scared me, and that I was about to cry.

Mom said, "No. It could be anybody in the whole family–you know, Shirl and Ethel's family, Rob and Goldie's family, or Jim and Hazel's. It could even be somebody not too close kin to us."

That was a relief because my little mind immediately placed

her prediction onto one of Aunt Gladys' kids whom I hadn't seen but one time. I felt much better. As long as I can remember, I had a way of dealing with much of the pain of my childhood. If I heard grown-ups say that someone was dying, I put a different name on the person so that the news didn't hurt me as much.

A day or so after Mom saw the white image coming around our house, I overheard her telling Grandma Molly and Aunt Goldie what she had seen. They both agreed with her that the white image was a sign that somebody was going to die. They went through their heads and speculated about who was sick.

Aunt Goldie said, "Well, you know Stella is not doing so good with her bleeding ulcers."

Mom thought about that for a moment and answered, "Could be, I reckon."

Grandma Molly chimed in, "It could be anybody. You know, Tom Crawford saw something white fly up out of the graveyard when he was comin' home from the moonshine still. The next day he saw Jesus standing on a rock. He was shot by a revenue man the day after that happened. You don't have to be sick to die."

A short while after Mom saw the white image come around the house, a catbird bird flew into the front window of our house and killed itself. I was on the cement-slab front porch playing with Larry and Brenda. The bird fell right in front of us. Mom heard the noise and came rushing out to see if we were all right. She asked, "What was that noise?" I pointed to the bird fluttering on the porch. She put her hand over her mouth and said, "Oh my God, somebody in the family is going to die." I was used to her predictions by this time, so it wasn't as scary. She picked the bird up off the porch and threw it in the back yard for the cats to eat.

Later in the afternoon, Mrs. May, who had the only phone for the community, knocked on our front door. Although she lived next door, Mrs. May was not a regular visitor to our house, so her appearance at the door was unusual. Mom opened the door. When she saw Mrs. May, she put her hand over her mouth and said, "Oh no. What's happened?"

Mrs. May answered, "Hattie's husband dropped dead while he was workin' on a car this afternoon. He had a heart attack. Somebody called Norman at work, and he called and asked me to tell you. I'm sorry Myrtle." Mrs. May turned around, and then she sluggishly walked back to her house.

Mom slowly closed the door. Hattie was my daddy's sister. She and her husband, Earl, had two little girls. Mom felt especially close to Earl and Hattie, because she and Dad had married at the same time that they did. Three couples had stood before the same preacher on July 27, 1940, and said their vows. Earl was only in his thirties. His death was a real shock to everyone.

When Dad arrived home from work that evening, Mom told him about the bird. "A cat bird flew into our bedroom window and killed itself this morning," she said. "I was expecting to get some bad news, but who would have thought it would be Earl? He is too young. What will Hattie do with those two little girls?"

Dad sat down to eat his supper, "I don't know how Hattie is gonna make it. I guess she'll have to learn to drive and go to work." After that, he became quiet and never lifted his head from his plate until he finished eating.

When death occurred in small and isolated Appalachian Mountain communities, it was noted by most members of the community because death occurred at home in the "living room" bed. Children were present and aware that a family member was seriously ill. They heard the discussions of the signs of death as the end drew near. They were often present as the last breath left the body. Therefore, children experienced death as just another part of life.

Chapter 14

My First Real Experiences with Death

I walked a mile with Pleasure;
She chattered all the way.
But left me none the wiser
For all she had to say.
I walked a mile with Sorrow
And ne'er a word said she;
But oh, the things
I learned from her
When Sorrow
walked with me!

Robert Browning

My first experience with death came when I was five years old. Aunt Goldie's husband, Uncle Rob, became ill. He often came to our house with severe pains in his stomach. He would hold his stomach as he climbed out of his car. When he came in the house, he asked, "Myrt, do you have any clabber? I am really sick."

Uncle Rob thought the problem was due to his ulcers and that Mom's slightly soured clabbered milk would soothe the pain.

Mom always had a dish of clabber on the back of the woodstove. She put the dish on the kitchen table, and Uncle Rob sat down at the table and ate it with a tablespoon.

One day Uncle Rob was in such pain that he came in from the sawmill and lay down across the "living room" bed. Aunt Goldie helped him take his work clothes off and covered him with a blanket. Uncle Rob told her to look in the top left pocket of his overalls. She found a roll of money. He told her he had just sold a lot of lumber and had $2,500 in his pocket. It was a small fortune in 1946.

In her frenzy to get her husband some help, Aunt Goldie forgot all about the money. She rushed the half mile to Mrs. May's house to have her call Dr. Watson. He came all the way from Broadway and examined Uncle Rob. Dr. Watson told him that he had gall bladder stones and needed an operation.

That evening, Mom and Dad talked about the upcoming surgery as being somewhat serious, but they also knew one or two people who had had their gall bladders removed. They didn't seem worried. Uncle Rob was a strong man and only thirty-six years old.

Uncle Rob went in for his surgery in the afternoon and the doctors operated on him the next day. The hospital told Aunt Goldie that he accidentally rolled out of bed after his surgery, and he died before the night was over. John I. Myers got the call from the hospital and rode his horse to Aunt Goldie's house and our house to bring us the terrible news.

Early in the morning, around 4:00 a.m., John I. Myers called my daddy's name from the road in front of the house. The call awoke me in the bed across the room. I looked toward the window and saw an image of a man on a horse. Mom said, "Wake up, Norman, its John I. Myers on his horse."

I felt the room fill with their fear as Mom whispered, "Oh no." She knew the news had to be bad because John I. Myers did not ride his horse at such an early hour. Mom and Dad got out of bed, slowly opened the front door, and walked out on the cement-slab front porch to get the bad news. From the back of his horse, Mr. Myers told them, "Rob Crawford passed away during the night."

Mom and Dad both screamed and cried as Mr. Myers slowly rode away on his horse. I started crying, too, because I had never seen Mom and Dad so upset. They told me, "Uncle Rob is dead." I was too young to understand what they meant. All I knew was that Uncle Rob was a special person to both Mom and Dad. He had married Aunt Goldie after her daddy died and left Mom an orphan at age nine. He and Aunt Goldie took Mom in and gave her a home until she married Dad.

Uncle Rob's passing was my first real experience with death. Unfortunately, it was also my first experience with the power of money to turn a friend or a relative into a thief. Some time while Uncle Rob was in the hospital or during the funeral, a friend or relative slipped into the downstairs bedroom and stole the $2,500 from his overalls pocket.

The undertaker brought Uncle Rob home in his casket and set him in the "sun" room that he had just finished building onto his and Aunt Goldie's house. I hung around and watched Aunt Goldie and Mom break down and cry. My cousins, Ruby, Joyce, Randy, and George all cried. I asked Mom, "Why are you all cryin'?"

She answered, "Because Uncle Rob is dead, and he is never coming back to life."

She turned to my daddy. "Norman, hold her up so she can see Rob in the casket. Let her touch his face," she said.

Dad picked me up and there was Uncle Rob looking like he was asleep. "Here, put your hand on his cheek," Dad said. I laid my hand on his face and quickly pulled it back. His face was hard and cold to touch. This was a shock because Uncle Rob was forever picking me up and kissing my cheeks, and he was always warm and soft.

"Wake him up, Daddy," I said.

Dad answered, "He can't wake up. He is gone to live in

heaven."

Uncle Rob laid in his casket for what seemed to me to be a long time. Meantime, every one of my relatives came to visit. Even Uncle Charlie and his whole family came down from Pennsylvania. Most everybody brought food so that Aunt Goldie didn't have to worry about feeding her family and the other relatives during this terrible time. However, one of these people also stole the money that Aunt Goldie needed desperately after the loss of her husband.

Every table in the house was cleared and made available for dishes of food–fried chicken, sliced ham, potato salad, sliced tomatoes, cakes, apple and peach pies, cole slaw and big pots of green beans fresh from gardens. Uncle Rob died on September 21–when gardens were producing their second bounty of green beans. Friends came with their own dishes and had something to eat from the buffet of food already there.

Finally, the undertaker came to take Uncle Rob to the cemetery for his burial. Mom agreed to stay at the house and watch the small children. I later learned that she didn't like to go to funerals because the red clay from the grave reminded her of her mother's death. For the remainder of her life, Mom never attended a funeral, including my dad's. On this day, she stood next to the stairway and watched as the undertakers wheeled Uncle Rob's casket to the front door. I clung to her leg and watched the tears run down her cheeks.

As the pallbearers picked up the casket to carry it down the step, across the front porch, and down the short walk to the waiting hearse, the sky opened and rain began to fall. Mom gasped. "Happy is the corpse that the rain falls on," she said as she saw the rain drops splash on top of Uncle Rob's coffin and gently run down the sides.

Several days after the funeral, Aunt Goldie remembered the money that Uncle Rob had had in his pocket. She went into the downstairs bedroom and found his overalls lying across the foot of the bed just as she had left them. She opened the upper left hand pocket and it was empty. The money was not there. She searched all the other pockets–no money to be found!

I became obsessed with Uncle Rob's death. For a long time after he was buried, Aunt Goldie and Mom went to visit his grave nearly every day. They took me along with them. I missed Uncle Rob and wanted to see him. When I stood at his grave, I tried to force my eyes to see through the dirt. I wondered what was happening down in the ground. "Is Uncle Rob rotten in his grave just like that cow that Dad drug up on the hills after she died?" I asked Mom.

Mom answered, "Well, we put him in a vault so he will look the same for a while. The vault keeps the water away from him, so he'll stay dry."

Meanwhile, Aunt Goldie was struggling with the fact that one of her friends or relatives had robbed her. "Who would have done such a thing?" she asked Mom. "I can't believe it. Maybe Rob got out of bed while I went to call the doctor and hid the money somewhere on the farm." She searched the house from top to bottom. She searched every outbuilding from the barn to the outdoor toilet. I went with her on some of these searches. She pulled out every loose board on every building and peered behind it to see if Uncle Rob had hidden the money there. Of course, she never found the money. To the moment of her death, she wondered who among Uncle Rob's and her friends and relatives could live with the fact that he or she had stolen the money she needed to raise her underage children.

Grandpa Austin Shifflett's Death

I don't remember any more deaths until I was fourteen years old. That was when Grandpa Austin died. He gave up living when he found his old white mule dead in the barn one morning. When he came in the house, he said, "My mule is dead. I have no reason to live." He immediately took off his clothes and lay down in the "living room" bed. It took him a full four years to die. Grandma Molly and Lena waited on him hand and foot. He wanted to die so badly that he fought them when they brought food to his bedside. He grabbed their arms and sunk his long fingernails into their flesh. Toward the end of his life, Aunt Lena had to hold him while Grandma Molly forced food into his mouth. He had no choice but to swallow it or choke.

Mom cut his hair when it grew too long, but Aunt Lena and Grandma Molly had to hold his hands while Mom snipped away at what little gray hair he had on the sides of his head. Mom always washed his head with soap and water when she finished cutting his hair. He died in that same bed in February 1958. A layer of snow had fallen the day before. It was cold and the wind howled outside the house. As soon as he took his last breath, Grandma Molly walked to the window and opened it. "We'll have to put up with the cold air for a while until his spirit gets out of the house," she said. She walked around the house, turned all the mirrors to the wall, and laid pictures down so that the faces were hidden from view.

Grandpa Austin was mean to us grandchildren and everybody else in the family when he was living. I never liked him. In fact, I called him Austin all the time as a way of refusing to acknowledge his important place in my life. I could not understand what the big "to do" was when he died. He was mean to Grandma Molly and Lena. He rarely spoke to them except to point at his pocket watch when it was time for them to start cooking a meal. He urinated off the front porch and made the front yard smell awful in the summer time. He spit tobacco juice all over the floor around the stove because he could not hit the spittoon. He seemed to hate his grandchildren. When we arrived after church on Sundays, he pulled his pocketknife out of his pocket, opened it, and pretended he was cutting our throats. He spit tobacco juice on our toes when we went barefoot in the summer time. The whole family fussed about him constantly when he was living. Mom complained about how he ate his meals. He piled bread on his plate, piled brown beans on top of it, and then added a layer of canned peaches. He gobbled it all up without saying a word. His forehead broke out in a sweat he ate so fast. He ate like it was his job. I never saw him laugh or smile. He frowned so much that his eyebrows hung down over his eyes.

Even as a younger man, Grandpa Austin's eyebrows hung low over his eyes. He seemed to be allergic to laughter.

After Grandpa Austin died, Grandma Molly and his daughters sat around and cried and talked about what a good person he was when he was living. In fact, everyone who came to the house talked about what a hardworking and good man he was. I was confused once more by this contradiction. I had to listen carefully to learn they were talking about Grandpa Austin. I was also confused about the pictures Dad took of him in his coffin. He never clicked the camera on Grandpa Austin while he was living.

Several hours after Grandpa Austin passed on, the McMullen Funeral Home came to get his body. Preparation of his body took a day. Meanwhile, Grandma Molly and Aunt Lena cleaned the house, took a bath, and dressed in their mourning clothes. Grandma Molly had known Grandpa Austin's death was eminent; therefore, she and Aunt Lena had bought black clothing to wear. Grandma was proud that she had found a pair of black stockings to go with her black dress.

The funeral home returned Grandpa Austin to his home to lie in the living room while his family and friends visited and offered their condolences to the family. His burial was delayed because some relatives had a long distance to travel for the funeral. The whole family took turns for two days sitting up with him around the clock. Aunt Hattie, Aunt Lena, and Aunt Vernie kept walking over to his casket to see if he was breathing. Aunt Vernie said, "I'll swear I can see his chest goin' up and down."

Grandma Molly (right) stands with Aunt Lena the day of Grandpa Austin's funeral. They are wearing the traditional black dress although Grandma Molly has her apron on to protect her dress while she helps to serve food. The kitchen table is set for visitors coming by to view the body and pay their respects.

Meanwhile, they told stories about people who had been buried alive. I remember one story about a woman who was buried alive. For some reason, her grave was later opened, and she had scratched the lining off the lid to her casket. I pictured this in my head–the poor woman screaming, tearing at the top of the casket, and finally dying in agony. Grandma Molly told a story of a man who was on his way to the cemetery when he suddenly raised the lid to his casket and asked, "What is going on here?"

The story of the woman gave me nightmares for years. "How do you know when a person is really dead?" I once asked Mom.

She answered, "Well, in the old days, people didn't really know, and that's why embalming is done now. They draw all the blood out of the body and put some kind of liquid in the veins. If a body is not really dead, embalming kills it, and it helps to preserve the body."

During the time that Grandpa Austin laid there, Grandma

Molly kept shoving wood into the living room stove until it was hard to breathe because the room was so hot. Mom whispered to me, "The man's gonna rot before they take him out of here. I can smell him now."

Up the hill past the chicken house, McMullen Funeral Home carried Grandpa Austin's coffin home. I remember watching as they struggled up the hill over the loose gravel. I thought, "This is the last time Austin will come home."

Several hours before his funeral, Mom walked over to the casket and looked down at him.

"Lena, come here," she said quietly.

Aunt Lena walked over to where Mom was standing. "Austin's mouth is open. Y'all have it way too hot in here," she whispered.

Aunt Hattie and Aunt Vernie jumped off their chairs and rushed to the coffin. They started crying, "Poppa ain't dead. He's tryin' to say somethin'."

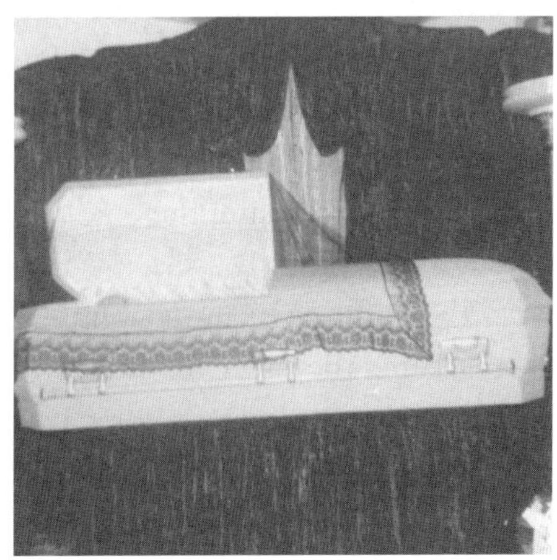

Grandpa Molly moved the "living room" bed out of the corner and placed Grandpa Austin in that spot. The funeral home placed a maroon drape behind his open coffin and over the pier on which his body sat for two days.

Soon after that, the funeral directors arrived to remove Grandpa Austin's body from the house and take it to the church. They saw that his mouth was open and stood between the casket and the family as they shut his mouth again.

The funeral director turned to me and asked, "Would you

be a flower girl for your granddaddy?"

My answer came out in the form of gasps and sobs. I could not stop crying.

Mom said to them, "I don't think she can carry his flowers."

Grandpa Austin's coffin is setting on top of his grave just before internment.

Grandpa Austin's sons–my daddy, Uncle Lurty, Uncle Floyd, and Uncle James–carried the coffin out of the house and placed it in the hearse for the short ride to the cemetery. The funeral service consisted of a sermon for the living and for Grandpa Austin. The preacher included remarks about the hardworking deceased and then switched to warn the living not to face death without repenting. Throughout the sermon, my aunts were sobbing. When the casket was closed and rolled down the isle of the church toward the door, Aunt Vernie jumped up and threw herself onto the coffin and then swooned into the arms of her grandson.

At the gravesite, the cold wind felt like it was going to cut through my skin. The closest family members sat under a tent with the coffin. My aunts continued to cry for their father. After a long time, the preacher stopped talking. Everyone got up from the chairs to greet those who had stood outside the tent. Aunt Vernie saw someone she knew and began walking up the hill to the parking lot. She was laughing and joking just as hard as she had just been crying in the church.

Later Mom asked me, "Why did you cry so hard when Mr. McMullen asked you to carry flowers? You always said you didn't like your granddaddy."

My answer surprised even me. "Well, I guess I really did like him. I miss him sometimes," I said.

Epilogue

For generations in the Appalachian Mountains, any newly married couple who established a home included a plan to have a "living room" bed near the stove. This piece of furniture was essential to family life before the invention of central heating. The "living room" bed served mountain families at the most important times of the family life cycle–birth, healing, and death. It remained a necessary piece of living room furniture for as long as homes were heated with wood or coal stoves.

A bed in the living room was never unique to Appalachian Mountain homes; but it served longer in the mountains because of the slow progress of central heating into isolated gaps and hollows.

◆◆◆◆◆◆◆◆◆◆◆◆◆◆◆◆◆◆◆◆◆◆◆◆◆◆◆◆◆◆◆◆◆◆

Central Heating . . .

It was not until 1885 that the nation burned more coal than wood. Prior to that time, the majority of homes in America were heated with wood burning brick fireplaces and derivatives of the cast iron Franklin stove, which was invented in 1742.

By the end of the nineteenth century, the invention of low-cost cast iron radiators brought central heating to America's homes. This system, often located in the basement, had a coal-fired boiler that delivered hot water or steam to radiators in every room. At about the same time, Dave Lennox built and marketed the industry's first riveted-steel coal furnace.

Without electricity and fans to move air, these early furnaces transported heat by using ducts to capture warm air as it rose from the basement furnace to the rooms above. These two methods dominated home central heating until 1935, when the introduction of the first coal-powered forced-air furnace used the power of an electric fan to distribute the heated air through ductwork within the home.

In the Appalachian Mountains, though, forty-one percent of homes were without central heat in 1960 compared to fifteen percent of homes outside the region. Thus, central heating did not reach the isolated Appalachian Mountain areas for another thirty years after the invention of the forced-air furnace. In addition, not all families in the mountains could afford central heating; therefore, some continued to use coal and wood stoves well into the 1970s. (14)

◆◆◆◆◆◆◆◆◆◆◆◆◆◆◆◆◆◆◆◆◆◆◆◆◆◆◆◆◆◆◆◆◆◆

By the 1970's, most mountain areas were accessible by automobile, which made medical care more readily available. Sick family members recovered in hospitals or clinics. The number of people dying at home declined. Family responsibility decreased with these important changes, and that, along with the increased use of central heating, lessened the need for a "living room" bed.

For children of my generation, born in the 1940s, our experience of the transition from the "living room" bed to homes with central heat and no similar piece of furniture depended on the degree of isolation and access to medical doctors and hospitals. We were born in the "living room" bed; we recovered from childhood illnesses in the "living room" bed; and we watched our grandparents die in the "living room" bed because they still lived in the isolated mountain hollows. However, the homes we established when we married were far more likely to have central heat.

When my mom and dad married in 1940 and "went housekeeping," as they called it, they had a bed near the heat from the living room stove. Over their fifty-four year marriage, Mom insisted that the bed be moved out of the living room. This resulted in regular arguments with Dad over the need for the "living room" bed. Cold-natured Dad liked to sleep near the fire. Warm-natured Mom liked a cold bedroom. Mom won that fight. We had a "living room" bed at important points in our family life–while Dad was in the army, when Mom had her two babies at home, and when members of the family were sick. We had one once again at the end of Mom's life.

Therefore, members of my generations who grew up along the Appalachian Mountains were privileged to experience the role of the "living room" bed in mountain family life. We watched the need for the "living room" bed decline with modern medicine and modern inventions. Pat, from Franklin County, Virginia, remembers her dad lying in his "living room" bed in 1969 during his last days. Just before he died, family members decided to take him to the hospital. At that moment, the "living room" bed lost its purpose to modern medicine.

I watched Grandpa Austin die in the "living room" bed. He went to bed to die in 1954 but lingered until 1958. Grandma Molly stated in 1971 that she was tired and ready to die. She lay down in the "living room" bed where she planned to remain until her death. We forced her to go to the hospital where she lived for just a few days. Again, the "living room" bed lost its purpose because we believed that modern medicine could save Grandma Molly.

Interestingly, when my mother was dying in 2001, she insisted that we bring her home to die. Mom ordered my sister, Brenda, and Hilda, my sister-in-law, to get her a bed for the living room. They rented a hospital bed and placed it in the living room. By this time, Mom had installed central heat in her home. She came home from the hospital and died three days later. Mom died in the "living room" bed even though she had resisted having one there throughout her marriage.

THE END

Footnotes

1. Burch, Druin. 2009. "When Childbirth was Natural and Deadly." Natural History Magazine 10 January.

2. Interview with Mrs. Eve Deegan. 2009. Summer.

3. Ritchie, Pat. 2007. "Midwives of Brocks Gap." Research.

4. Lothrop, H. 1998. Breastfeeding Naturally. Fisher Books, USA.

5. "What St. Paul Wrote About Women." Selected passages from the New Testament. http://www.beliefnet.com/Faiths/Christianity/2004/03/What

6. Frey, Dorothy. 1984. "Vapo-Cresoline lamp cured many ills."

7. Engs, Ruth C. 2005. The Eugenics Movement: An Encyclopedia. Westport, CT: Greenwood Publishing Group.

8. "Plasters, Poultices and Paregoric: The Civil War Medicinal Cookbook." 2009. Civil War Interactive. http://www.civilwarinteractive.com/PoulticePlasterParegoric.htm.

9. Ackerknecht, Erwin Heinz.1982. A short history of medicine. Baltimore: Johns Hopkins University Press.

10. Dunaway, Wilma A. 2008. *Women, Work and Family in the Antebellum Mountain South.* Cambridge University Press.

11. "May Day Customs." 2009. http://www.theholidayspot.com/mayday/customs.htm

12. Hancock, Norma. 1954. "Shivarees." *Western Folklore*, Vol. 14, No. 2, pp. 136-137.

13. Van Gennep, Arnold.1909; 1960. *The rites of passage*. Chicago: University of Chicago Press.

14. "A Brief History of Heating and Cooling America's Homes." 2007. http://sunhomedesign.wordpress.com/2007/10/26/a-brief-history-of-heating-and-cooling-americas-homes/